A PLUME BOOK

THE BIG JEWISH BOOK FOR JEWS

Courtesy of author

Susan Burnstine

ELLIS WEINER and BARBARA DAVILMAN are authors of *Yiddish with Dick and Jane*, *Yiddish with George and Laura*, *How to Raise a Jewish Dog*, *How to Profit from the Coming Rapture*, *Arffirmations: Meditations for Your Dog*, and *Catechisms: Fundamentals of Feline Faith*.

Ellis, solo, is author of, among other books, *Decade of the Year*, *The Joy of Worry*, *Drop Dead, My Lovely*, *The Big Boat to Bye-Bye*, *Santa Lives! Five Conclusive Arguments for the Existence of Santa Claus*, and *Oy! Do This, Not That!*

Barbara is coeditor, with Liz Dubelman, of *What Was I Thinking?*

They are married (to each other) and live in Los Angeles.

THE
BIG JEWISH BOOK
FOR JEWS

Everything You Need to Know
to Be a Really Jewish Jew

Ellis Weiner and
Barbara Davilman

A PLUME BOOK

PLUME
Published by Penguin Group

Penguin Group (USA) Inc., 375 Hudson Street, New York, New York 10014, U.S.A. • Penguin Group (Canada), 90 Eglinton Avenue East, Suite 700, Toronto, Ontario, Canada M4P 2Y3 (a division of Pearson Penguin Canada Inc.) • Penguin Books Ltd., 80 Strand, London WC2R 0RL, England • Penguin Ireland, 25 St. Stephen's Green, Dublin 2, Ireland (a division of Penguin Books Ltd.) • Penguin Group (Australia), 250 Camberwell Road, Camberwell, Victoria 3124, Australia (a division of Pearson Australia Group Pty. Ltd.) • Penguin Books India Pvt. Ltd., 11 Community Centre, Panchsheel Park, New Delhi – 110 017, India • Penguin Books (NZ), 67 Apollo Drive, Rosedale, North Shore 0632, New Zealand (a division of Pearson New Zealand Ltd.) • Penguin Books (South Africa) (Pty.) Ltd., 24 Sturdee Avenue, Rosebank, Johannesburg 2196, South Africa

Penguin Books Ltd., Registered Offices: 80 Strand, London WC2R 0RL, England

First published by Plume, a member of Penguin Group (USA) Inc.

First Printing, August 2010

10 9 8 7 6 5 4 3 2 1

Ⓟ REGISTERED TRADEMARK—MARCA REGISTRADA

LIBRARY OF CONGRESS CATALOGING-IN-PUBLICATION DATA

Weiner, Ellis.
    The big Jewish book for Jews : everything you need to know to be a really Jewish Jew / Ellis Weiner and Barbara Davilman.
        p. cm.
    ISBN 978-0-452-29644-2
  1. Jewish wit and humor.   2. Jews—Identity.   3. Jews—Social life and customs. 4. Judaism—Customs and practices.   5. Jews—Anecdotes.   I. Davilman, Barbara. II. Title.
    PN6231.J5W44 2010
    818'.5402—dc22
                                                                              2010011187

Printed in the United States of America
Set in ITC Galliard

PUBLISHER'S NOTE

BOOKS ARE AVAILABLE AT QUANTITY DISCOUNTS WHEN USED TO PROMOTE PRODUCTS OR SERVICES. FOR INFORMATION PLEASE WRITE TO PREMIUM MARKETING DIVISION, PENGUIN GROUP (USA) INC., 375 HUDSON STREET, NEW YORK, NEW YORK 10014.

To Marsha Weiner
and
Andrew Davilman,
who were there, too.

Contents

Acknowledgments

Thanks to:

Adam Abramowicz for speed, accuracy, and patience in the execution of the original art. As usual.

INTRODUCTION

A young rabbi, recently installed in a synagogue, is informed by the *shamos* that the building has rats. They call this exterminator and that exterminator but nothing works. The rats remain. Finally the rabbi, at the end of his rope, calls the previous rabbi, who has retired to Arizona. The young man explains the problem and the elder rabbi says, "Ah, yes. I've heard of this problem at a different *shul*. Here's what you do. Wait in the sanctuary until the next time the rats come out. When they do, perform a Bar Mitzvah service for all of them. Believe me, after that, you'll never see them again."

Thus, what we might call "The Rabbi's Lament"—that once a Jewish child is Bar (or Bat) Mitzvah, the child quits Hebrew school and loses all interest in his or her religion. And so do the parents. Maybe they continue to attend services for High Holy Days, but after a while, not even.

You may be such a person, or you may know someone who is. We're talking about Jews who:

- Show up for work one day and wonder why the place is deserted. When they ask, it's up to the Gentiles in the office to explain that it's Yom Kippur.
- Have a Christmas tree in their living room "because it's festive."
- Respect their children as individuals and accept their fashion choices.
- When they have to call a doctor, have to look up the number.
- Stop eating when they're full.
- Respond to hearing the phone ring by picking it up and saying, "Hello?" with neither despair nor panic.

These kinds of behaviors are increasingly common among American Jews. Never mind the problems posed by intermarriage, resurgent anti-Semitism, investment frauds, and controversy over support for Israel; the direst threat to Judaism in the U.S. today is its very success.

There is not one facet of American life in which Jews have not made significant contributions and attained appreciable power and prestige, from the arts and entertainment, to business and finance, to the sciences and medicine, academia, politics, fashion, cuisine, and law. Jews have even made their mark in evangelical Christianity; several of that movement's most influential figures were once Jews who—go know why, go understand people and their *meshugass*—converted.

But this very success threatens to bring about the undoing of American Jewishness itself, because Jewish achievement in the U.S. has been inseparable from secular assimilation. The more Americanized we become—the more we find it acceptable to order pastrami on white, to elope to Vegas instead of throwing a wedding comparable to the coronation of Queen Beatrix of the Netherlands, or to play (or to know people who play) polo—the less *Jewish* we are.

And the less Jewish we *feel*. A gaping chasm opens in the center of our identity. When we turn inward to draw strength and sustenance from the most fundamental aspects of our selves, and we open the part of our heart marked "Jewish," we find nothing there, except maybe a little Post-it that says, "I used to watch *Seinfeld*."

And then there are the young people, the new generation of cool Jews who think they've got it all figured out. Perhaps you know (or even are!) one of them, someone who:

- Drinks hip Jewish beers like Miller Chai Life, Schnoors Light, and Bubmeisen.
- Attends Confirmation services at Reform synagogues wearing jeans and a T-shirt, or a sweat suit or, in certain climates, in anticipation of the Underwater Oneg Shabbat to follow the service, scuba gear.
- Sports tattoos, in "Hebraic" English letters, reading CHOSEN or OY MEETS WORLD.

- Puts a suction cup sign on the window of your hybrid car that says BUBBIE ON BOARD or a bumper sticker that asks HOW'S MY DAVENING?
- Listens to and attends concerts by Jewish rock artists such as NU 2, Fifty Shek, and Bruce Springsteenstein.

All this coolness, and yet . . .

Something doesn't feel right. In spite of all the hip Jewish trappings, the proud assertion of a contemporary Jewish identity, the Jewishness flaunted at every possible opportunity, this person *doesn't feel Jewish.*

But how could they, when this "celebration" of Jewishness is merely a matter of style, of consumer goods and fashion and taste, as doomed to obsolescence as last year's cell phones?

This, then, is the reality of contemporary, non-Orthodox Judaism in America. The young advertise a paper-thin Jewishness with consumer choices and tattoos, like a bunch of hoodlums. The middle-aged and older abandon all traditional practices and can't be bothered to go on the Sisterhood's New York Matinee Outing to see *South Pacific,* let alone attend services.

The more established, accomplished, and assimilated older Jews have become, the more "being Jewish" feels no different from "being normal." And the more with-it, cool, groovy, dope, and "da bomb" being Jewish has become for the young generation, the more it is indistinguishable from plain old being American.

No wonder, then, a burning issue has seized the imaginations of American Jewry. You, your relatives, your friends—everyone is plagued by a single dilemma, whether they know it or not: *"How can we regain a sense of what it really means to be Jewish?"*

That's why you have picked up this book, and that's why we have written it.

We want to keep Judaism from disappearing into the melting pot of all-American fabulousness. We want to save it from its own secular success and, in this way, restore to the reader a sense of religious and ethnic identity that no amount of gourmet rosemary-infused matzoh or reruns of *Curb Your Enthusiasm* can provide.

How? By preserving certain practices and beliefs hitherto held sacred, or at least important, or at least fun, by the generations that have come before, lest they atrophy from neglect or become entirely forgotten.

In the pages that follow, we will do this by reminding, educating, and instructing you in the traditional ways, the ways of our ancient Hebraic ancestors and of our mothers, fathers, and some of our aunts. We will remind you how to do the kinds of things your parents may have done but have failed to transmit to you, such as building an ark. We will review the rich panoply of Jewish culture to which you may have become oblivious, concerning such topics as *tefillin*, pickles, and *Fiddler*.

We will, in short, help you to rediscover your own Jewishness by reconnecting with the old rituals and ideas, the ones that flourished between the late Bronze Age and the 1950s. It was during this interval— roughly delineated by the Exodus from Egypt and the Beatles' appearance on *The Ed Sullivan Show*—when everyone knew what it meant to be Jewish, and felt it, and maybe sometimes *kvetched* about it.

In the following pages, then, we invite you on a journey—a journey of discovery and, maybe, just maybe, just maybe maybe, of self-discovery. Come. Read. Enjoy. Try it. You'll like it. It couldn't hurt. Ready? Begin.

Some Conventions

We will employ certain conventions in the text. We will, per Orthodox tradition, spell in English the name of the Lord as "G-d," except when reproducing quotes from other sources that use the conventional spelling. And we will use the abbreviations BCE (Before the Common Era) and CE (Common Era) instead, respectively, of BC and AD.

E.W.
B.D.
Los Angeles

THE
BIG JEWISH BOOK
FOR JEWS

1

"Just in Case"

efore anything else—before learning Yiddish, making chopped liver, wearing *tefillin*, or plunging into Mah-Jongg—if you want to renew your Jewishness you have to grasp, and use in ways you may have never used before, the phrase "just in case."

It means exactly what you think it means: "in the event of some unforeseen misfortune," "as a safeguard against some bad thing," and so on. But it means more than that. Compare these two statements made by two individuals about to leave, to attend a baseball game at the stadium:

A. "I'm bringing an umbrella to the game, just in case."
B. "I'm bringing a poncho, a pair of lightweight rubber boots, a flask of brandy, a tin of ibuprofen pills and antibiotic capsules, a waterproof ski mask, an emergency flare, an umbrella, and a tent, and I'm wearing a wet suit under my clothes to the game, just in case."

The difference should be obvious. In Statement A, the speaker, in acknowledging the possibility of rain, is blithely ignoring the equal possibility of a tornado. The speaker of Statement B knows better than to tempt fate in such a way, and—equally "just in case"—announces himself to be properly equipped.

As this example demonstrates, just knowing how to say "just in case" isn't enough, because you never know, and something could "happen." So you have to take steps, and be extra careful, and provide for redundant measures of safety and making-sure in whatever you do.

Naturally, the question then arises: With regard to what should I take these extreme measures of safety and concern? The answer is simple: With regard to everything. It sounds overwhelming, and if you do it right, it *is* overwhelming. But why shouldn't you be overwhelmed a little, just in case?

For example, take the universally understood dilemma of going to an airport. Everyone knows that the official recommendation to passengers traveling on a domestic flight in the United States is to arrive at the terminal ninety minutes before departure time. The reasons, too, are well known: Security measures and cost-cutting moves of the airlines often result in long lines, bottlenecks, delays, and inconveniences, so the earlier you get there, the less chance there is of you missing your flight.

This kind of thinking is all well and good for the devil-may-care, go-with-the-flow non-Jews among the flying public, but Jews—*Real* Jews—know that ninety minutes before departure is the time, ideally, you'd want to be boarding the aircraft, if they would only let you. They won't, for reasons we needn't go into, but the fact remains that you should insist on arriving at the airport *at least three hours before the recommended ninety-minute arrival time,* just in case.

There is a dual reason for this, as indeed there is a dual reason behind everything we do "just in case." The first has its basis in practicality: We don't want to miss our flight—indeed, who does?—and so we elect to arrive at the airport five hours before the plane we will be boarding is scheduled to depart the airport it will be departing prior to landing at ours to disgorge its passengers and be readied for our flight.

But behind this outwardly obvious concern lies the second, more hidden but no less potent, reason: It's the only way to manage our anxiety. It need hardly be said that to be Jewish is to live with anxiety, in the same way that to be a trout is to live with water. Our anxiety, like all true anxiety, is infinite and all-encompassing. We know, even if no one else does, that:

- The world is full of maniacs.
- You never know what can happen.
- Unanticipated occurrences take place and what can you do?
- Certain emergencies arise.
- Other people aren't as responsible as we are.
- Just driving down the street, you're surrounded by lunatics.
- The weather is very unpredictable.
- Something could go wrong with the car.
- If there's a bomb scare somewhere, everything stops and you're dead.
- The parking lots, it's a free-for-all, you could get killed.
- With the highways falling apart, and the roadwork, and the tumult, you end up getting detoured through Timbuktu.
- Other things you shouldn't even think about.

It's a formidable list of potential hazards, and you'd have to be out of your mind to ignore it. Jews, an oppressed minority from before Moses, even, have ample reasons for fearing the worst, and an extensive history of being subjected to it.

That's why we take a sweater to go bowling (the air-conditioning may be too cold), insist that the children wear life jackets on a Disneyland Jungle Cruise (the boat might capsize), and stick with the tour group when sightseeing in London (England Shmengland, it's a foreign country).

Someone might object and call this attitude "irrational." We say: You're darn right it is—because the world is dangerous, and danger is irrational. We can pat ourselves on the back for all the brilliant, ultra-rational intellectuals and scientists who have emerged from the Children of Israel over the centuries, but remember: It's not for nothing that we have a Yiddish expression (*Kain ein horeh!*) for warding off the Evil Eye.

Think of "just in case" like that, as a magical incantation to repel bad luck. But don't just say it. *Do* it—meaning, take steps to proactively defend against the possibility of everything. Because you never know.

2

HOW TO PURCHASE, MAKE, AND SERVE TOO MUCH FOOD

The American-Jewish tradition of making and serving too much food—and oppressing your guests with stated or implied commands to eat it—goes back to time immemorial, meaning about a hundred years ago. To the Jews who arrived in America in the early twentieth century, serving too much food during holidays and celebrations symbolized two contrasting but oddly congruent things.

For the prosperous middle- and upper-middle class who emigrated from Germany, too much food functioned as a visible embodiment of their worldly success. For the lower-class Jewish immigrants from Eastern Europe and Russia, too much food served as a symbol of hope, of an abundance to come now that they had arrived in the Land of Opportunity.

Sadly, however, over the decades, the practice of making a ton of food and being offended if people don't eat forty-seven times their weight in it has fallen into disrepute. The Jewish holiday table has become Americanized, with cooks using less fat, salt, and sugar in dishes featuring a wide range of fresh and even exotic ingredients, and with their guests hurtfully taking sensible portions of it and not lapsing into diabetic comas or suffering myocardial incidents after one light, refreshing (as opposed to four suffocating) dessert(s).

No wonder American Jews don't feel as Jewish as they used to. They eat like Protestants—and, worse, still drink like Jews. They "enjoy," if that's the word, the worst of both worlds. But fortunately, such bad habits can be broken and a new (i.e., old) regime of food preparation and service can be learned.

All it takes is the will to buy too much food, to prepare too much food, to serve too much food, to insist that your guests eat most if not all of it, and, if any is left over, to compel those who have not been rushed to the emergency room to take home with them a "doggie bin" of leftovers "for tomorrow." Here's how.

How to Purchase Too Much Food

The secret to purchasing too much food lies in chanting, quietly or even silently, to yourself the simple Jewish mantra "just in case."

Equipped with your shopping list, you stand before each section of the supermarket and select the items you need for the amount of each dish you are planning, consistent with the number of guests you expect. Then, just before leaving that section to go to the next one, pause. Say to yourself, "I'd better get a little more," and then recite the mantra, "just in case." Then select again exactly as much of each item as you already have.

Thus, in each case, you will be buying twice as much as you "need."

When employing this technique for the first time, you may be tempted to ask yourself, "Just in case of what? We're trapped in the house by a snowstorm? The Baltimore Ravens' offensive line shows up for dinner? Someone steals half my groceries in the parking lot?"

These questions, while sensible, are irrelevant. Purchasing too much food is not a rational activity, and is not subject to reasonable challenges. It's a religio-cultural activity, and is driven by faith—the faith that you'd better buy and make too much, just in case.

How to Make Too Much Food

No doubt when you were studying fractions in elementary school and one inquisitive student asked, "Why are we learning this? Will we ever actually use it in real life?" the teacher offered various examples of the utility of fractions, one of which was inevitably the prospect of wanting to make just part of a recipe. "Say you're cooking for two people. If your recipe serves four people and calls for half a pint of cream, you'll need fractions to know how much cream to use."

Well, good news. When making too much food, we're not talking about pesky dividing. We're talking about multiplying, usually whole numbers starting with 2 and going as high as necessary.

Rules for Serving Too Much Food

PREPARATION

1. Do not make an *amuse-bouche*.
In finer restaurants an *amuse-bouche* (lit. "mouth-amuser," also called an *amuse-gueule*) is a sort of pre-appetizer. Forget it. You're not about to amuse anyone's *bouche*. You are going to dominate every damn *bouche* at the table.

2. Serve lots of bread.
Before, during, and after the meal. Bread bread bread. And butter. And a dish of margarine, because some people are "on a diet."

3. Regarding the main dish: Always make twice as much as the recipe requires for its specified number of servings if convenient with regard to buying the ingredients. If it's not convenient, make three times as much.
This deceptively simple formula is surprisingly powerful.

Above, you learned how to shop for too much food, and it was suggested you buy twice as much as you "need." Note, here, that in many cases what you originally intended to buy did not exactly match the requirements of your recipes. Say, you needed half a cup of brown sugar to make baked sauerkraut. You had no brown sugar in the house, so you were stuck having to buy an entire box of it—and then, after chanting "just in case," you ended up buying two boxes.

You don't need to make enough baked sauerkraut so that you succeed in using both entire boxes of brown sugar. That would be absurd. But if you have ended up with more than twice as much as you need *of a fundamental ingredient,* use it all.

Say, for example, your recipe for Pot Roast with Winter Kale and Poached Apricots calls for a three-pound slab of beef chuck to serve eight. If you can conveniently get a six-pound slab of chuck (or two three-pound, or three two-pound, steaks), do so. If the available chuck steaks don't easily equal six pounds, you may have ended up having to buy seven pounds or more. (Remember this is for the original eight people.) *Make all of it,* not just the called-for minimum of six pounds. As long as it's going to be inconvenient, you might as well go all the way.

Naturally, you will have to double or even triple, as the case may be, all the other ingredients in the pot roast recipe.

DIETARY NOTE: You may be aware of the dietary needs of your guests, or you may be unaware of them. Don't worry about it. In either case, in the above example, serve a couple of chickens, "just in case" some people don't eat beef.

4. Always double the amount of every side dish, appetizer, condiment, and salad.

Note, here, that while you should make *more* than double the amount of the main course you prepare, you need only to *double* everything else. Why? Because you need to be able to tell your guests to "save room for dessert."*

SERVING

1. Present everything "family style," in large serving bowls and on huge platters.

This, rather than assembling individual plates in the kitchen. You

---

You don't really want them to save room for dessert. You don't want them to even save room to breathe. You want them to eat dessert while in a semiconscious state of overwhelmed satiety. But holding back on the side dishes—making available merely twice as much as anyone can consume—allows you to pretend to your guests that you think they're still hungry and eager for more.

want everyone to be overwhelmed visually by the abundance of food, and physically intimidated by the prospect of having to eat it all.

2. Act coy and naughty, as though you and your guests are getting away with something.

Imply, in your manner, that eating this well (or, at least, this much) is "really" a forbidden pleasure and a "decadent" indulgence. The idea is to pretend that you are your own great-great-grandparent, and that both you and your guests have just trudged in from the landowner's potato fields—as opposed to what you are, i.e., contemporary Americans with ready access to a good diet and a fantastic variety of foods from all over the world. This will underscore the religious and cultural meaning of the occasion.

3. Verbally bully everyone into taking more.

Don't be afraid to contradict them outright. If X says, "Thanks, but I'm full," be openly disbelieving and reply, "Oh, you are not! Here, I'll serve you myself."

4. Always hold some massive additional dish in reserve.

Lay out all platters and bowls *except one* before summoning people to the table. Let everyone get settled. Be modestly silent as people express amazement at the variety of dishes and disbelief at their staggering quantities. Encourage the passing of the food in various directions and prompt everyone to take at least twice as much as they wish to take.

Then, just before people start eating and everyone has (they think) reconciled themselves to what will be required of them, suddenly say, in an urgent whisper, "Oh my G-d, I forgot the ____." Rush back into the kitchen and emerge with as gigantic a bowl of something—mashed sweet potatoes, string beans, braised chicken thighs, ten tons of kasha, etc.—as possible. Make a place on the table for it with an absolute maximum of fuss, noise, and the clanging of colliding dishware. Refuse offers of help. Make it clear, by gesture and word, that you're going to all this bother *for them*; the least they can do in return is eat until they explode.

5. Serve at least three desserts and then serve little cookies.
Present these desserts with the same transgressive little wink that you used during the main service. Better yet, leer openly and imply that the whole dessert course is vaguely obscene and pornographic. Tease people who take servings; grow offended by and concerned with those who do not.

By following the above steps, you'll restore dinner to what it used to be—a celebration of immoral excess—and, in so doing, revitalize your traditional Jewish instincts.

Bon appétit!
You'll need it.

"Who wants six tons of peas and pearl onions while they're eating more bread?!"

3

HOW TO CHANGE YOUR NAME

First, a little quiz. Match the given Jewish name with the sleeker, less Jewish stage name:

Given Jewish Name	Sleeker, Less Jewish Stage Name
1. Bernice Frankel	a. Lenny Bruce
2. Shirley Schrift	b. Lee J. Cobb
3. Joseph Abraham Gottlieb	c. Tony Curtis
4. Melvin Kaminsky	d. Lee Grant
5. Leonard Alfred Schneider	e. Edward G. Robinson
6. Aaron Chwatt	f. Tony Randall
7. Edward Israel Iskowitz	g. Laurence Harvey
8. Melvin Edouard Hesselberg	h. Lauren Bacall
9. Leon Jacob	i. Joan Rivers
10. Bernard Schwartz	j. Peter Lorre
11. Jacob Cohen	k. Bea Arthur
12. Issur Danielovitch	l. Rodney Dangerfield
13. Lyova Haskell Rosenthal	m. Shelley Winters
14. Zvi Mosheh (Hirsh) Skikne	n. Judy Holliday
15. Judith Tuvim	o. Mel Brooks
16. Laszlo Lowenstein	p. Melvyn Douglas
17. Arthur Leonard Rosenberg	q. Eddie Cantor

18. Joan Alexandra Molinsky	r. Red Buttons
19. Emmanuel Goldenberg	s. Kirk Douglas
20. Betty Joan Perske	t. Joey Bishop

(Answers: 1 k; 2 m; 3 t; 4 o; 5 a; 6 r; 7 q; 8 p; 9 b; 10 c; 11 l; 12 s; 13 d; 14 g; 15 n; 16 j; 17 f; 18 i; 19 e; 20 h)

How Many Did You Get Right?

   0–5 *"A glick hot dich getrofen!"* ("Big deal!")
   6–10 *"Gantseh megilleh!"* ("Big deal!")
   10–15 *"Groisseh gedilleh!"* ("Big deal!")
   15–20 *"Zol vaksen tzibbelis fun pipek."* ("Onions should grow from your belly button.")

After taking this quiz, if you're like most people today under the age of, say, forty, your first question is, "Who's Red Buttons?" If you're older, your question is, "Wait—Joey *Bishop*? He was Jewish? Why not go all the way and call yourself Joey Pope?"

Okay, so much for your questions. The point is, one way to return to the traditional ways of the Jewish people is to change your name and go into show business.

Or change your name and *don't* go into show business. The important thing is to change your name.

Of course, those who did go into show business demonstrated, for the rest of us and for all time, how it's done. The list of Jews who molted their ethnic-sounding monikers and took on something more "American" is long and illustrious, encompassing everyone from the sublime (Winona Ryder = Winona Laura Horowitz) to the literally ridiculous (the Three Stooges, Larry Fine, Moe Howard, and Curly Howard = Laurence Feinberg, Moses Horwitz, and Jerome Lester Horwitz). Not to mention Michael "Bonanza" "Little House on the Prairie" "Highway to Heaven" Landon (= Eugene Maurice Orowitz).

We bring this up because today, for some reason, ethnic and angular and odd is "in." Actors who, two generations ago, would have changed their names before even getting their SAG cards, today swan around under the exact names they were given at birth!

Early talent agent renames two starlets. "Leah Rosenberg? Honey, from today on you're Lee Rome. Esther Greenspan? Oh, please. How about Evelyn Green?"

For example, take Zeljko Ivanek. Sure, he's a great actor (and may or may not be Jewish), but would it have killed him to give those of us trying to pronounce his name a break, and call himself Zeke Evans?

It seems paradoxical, or nuts, to suggest that you can become more Jewish by adopting a less Jewish name. But that's the *point*. The Jews from previous generations possessed a connection with their Jewishness to such a degree that they felt it necessary to conceal it when they became public figures in largely non-Jewish America.

In other words, *changing your name* is the way to recapture that first- or second-generation American Jewish spirit. It's easy, it's fun, and it probably costs only a few bucks to do it legally down at the courthouse or at City Hall or at AAA or the DMV or wherever one does such things.

If you feel like going easy on yourself, your family, and everyone who has ever met you, your new name can closely mimic your "real" name. The best example of this, in history and probably for the rest of all time, is the transformation (if you can call it that) from Leon Jacob to Lee J. Cobb.

At the opposite end of the spectrum is a new name (e.g., Lauren Bacall) that has absolutely nothing to do with the original (Betty Joan Perske).

So find your new name somewhere between those two extremes. Of course, back in the Golden Age of Changing Movie Stars' Names, the studios had P.R. experts to choose the new ones. That craft has, sadly, died out. To assist you, here are a few suggestions:

1. **Rhythm is important.** You are choosing, in essence, a brand name, an entity consisting of two halves that will be more or less inseparable. (We honor this when we describe the plot of a movie to someone. "Then Harrison Ford takes a plane to Cairo, and he has lunch with George Clooney," etc.) So be sure the meter of your first and last names, when they are combined, is pleasing. Don't just pick a first name and last name because, individually, you like them. They have to go together.

2. **Shorter is better than longer.** Not every name need be as punchy as "Mel Brooks" or "Gayle Storm." But aim for concision.

3. **Your adopted first name can evoke your real name, but it doesn't have to.** From Lyova to Lee, from Edward to Eddie: fine. But don't kill yourself. "Tony Curtis" bears no relation to "Bernard Schwartz," but it worked fine.

4. **If you want to go all the way, steer clear of actual names.** You're striving for artificiality and contrivance—you *want* people to know your name is made up. The only reason we didn't put Rock

Hudson or Tab Hunter in the previous quiz is that we assumed they weren't Jewish. Moreover, the distinction between male and female first names is rapidly disappearing. From Alex to Stevie to Sam to Evan, there is almost no male name that has not been adapted for female use. So just forget regular names entirely.

5. Don't be afraid of actual gibberish. Short, blunt nouns are okay, but nonsense words, baby talk, or sound effects can be especially effective in getting people to think, "Wow, with an obviously phony name like BOPP CRAGGER, GANT KOXMAN, or CHANQUE DOOGLAH, he must really be Jewish!"

Big Jewish Book for Jews Name-O-Matic

(Pick any name from Column A if male, from Column B if female; then pick any name from Column C.)

A First Names, Male	B First Names, Female	C Last Names
Ack	Ahn	Abs
Agamemnon	Ashley	Axton
Ark	Brannae	Babben
Balt	Bibi	Badams
Berton	Bijah	Baxton
Bob	Brellin	Belton
Bopp	Brenne	Blannade
Brik	Callay	Burk
Cam	Corelle	Cragger
Carper	Dahllyah	Crandall
Chanque	DeeDee	Crendall
Chip	Donnatella	Drake
Dack	Dulcie	Douglas
Dirk	Debb	DuGlah
Duck	Eelie	Ect
Erg	Evonne	Exton

(continued)

A First Names, Male	B First Names, Female	C Last Names
Fod	Feene	Fracture
Frak	Felisa	Fistt
Gant	Galeena	Galter
Grip	Genelle	Heaven
Hak	Hahllee	Horp
Hamp	Heathre	Isperdale
Igan	Ink	Ivens
Ive	Ixnee	Jonez
Jet	Jella	Joans
Jump	Jelleau	Jownes-Jemmz
Jute	Jenga	Klobbersmith
Kamp	Kohlrabi	Koxman
Krell	Kee	Levee
Linc	LahLee	Lillypond
Lon	Lezzenda	Lyntette
Ludd	Lorrall	Mint
Magner	Lycene	Moon-River
Mix	Marie-Marie	Mumms
Mudley	Mercerie	Nacelle
Nak	Mortadella	Nice
Nedley	Nellelle	Ninnie
Nik	Numatique	Noxon
Pack	Panzee	Parker
Piker	Philately	Porter
Prance	Pummisse	Parker-Porter
Quart	Py	Pthomas
Quill	Pyxxie	Quam
Rinc	Rielle	Racker
Russ	Rellie	Rigg
Sherk	Sha	Sacker
Stick	Sintilla	Savanne
Swagg	Swanne	Spoon
(etc.)	(etc.)	(etc.)

4

THE TEMPLES

It would be nice to think that, in your quest to renew your Jewish identity, you could make a pilgrimage to the absolute epicenter of the religion and rededicate yourself at Square One. This would entail traveling to Israel, making your way to Jerusalem, and arriving by cab, donkey, or foot at the entrance of the Temple, the Holy House itself. And you can! Mostly.

Israel is there, and so is Jerusalem. However, you'd be a bit (1,940 years) late for the Temple. The Romans destroyed it—the Second Temple—in 70 CE and, what with one thing and another (the Roman Empire; Egyptian Mamluk rule), and this and that (the Ottoman Empire; the rise of Islam), they haven't gotten around yet to rebuilding it.

The Second Temple was itself built on the ruins of the First, called Solomon's Temple, finished in 960 BCE—or so says the Bible. The Talmud disagrees, as it does with the reputed year of the Temple's destruction. The Bible says it was destroyed in 586 BCE; the Talmud, in 420 BCE. Either way, we're talking about a building that is supposed to have existed for four hundred years before it was obliterated by the Babylonians.

The Temple's purpose was to house the Ark of the Covenant, to function as the central headquarters for the Jewish people's worship, and to be the site of animal and other sacrifices. The only sources we have for determining its design are books of the Bible, including Joshua, Judges, 1–2 Samuel, and 1–2 Kings. But some of these accounts are pretty detailed, e.g., this, from 1 Kings 6:

> *In the inner sanctuary (Solomon) made two cherubim of olive-wood, each ten cubits high. Five cubits was the length of one wing of the cherub, and five cubits the length of the other wing of the cherub; it was ten cubits from the tip of one wing to the tip of the other.*

In 586 BCE the Jews were exiled to Babylon and the Temple razed. This was first of two Diasporas (dispersions), in which the Jews were exiled from their native land.

Solomon's Temple. One can only begin to imagine the splendor of the gift shop.

In 538 BCE the Persian Empire, under Cyrus the Great, defeated the Babylonians and permitted the Jews to return to Israel, where construction of a new Temple began in 535 BCE and was completed in 516 BCE. And then, in 19 BCE, Herod the Great tore the whole thing down and, adhering to the original ground plan, rebuilt it, spiffing it up with a new Greco-Roman facade. But this, which is sometimes called Herod's Temple, is still referred to as the Second Temple because its function as a site of sacrifices was uninterrupted throughout the renovation.

Finally, in 66 CE, the Jews revolted against the Roman Empire. Four years later, the Roman general Titus led an army into Jerusalem, sacked the city, and destroyed the Temple. The Jews again fled, creating the second Diaspora.

It was a trauma from which Judaism has never recovered. The building itself, by all accounts an exquisite feat of design and workmanship, was also an embodiment of unity for the Jewish people. Its destruction, therefore, was, and remains, just as symbolic. For years afterward, whenever a house or synagogue was built, it was the custom to leave a square yard of it unfinished, and inscribed with the Hebrew words meaning, "In memory of the Destruction."

Orthodox Jews believe that a Third Temple will be built on this same site, to coincide with the arrival of the Messiah. However, that may be more problematic than ever.

Since the late seventh century CE, the site has been occupied by the Dome of the Rock, an Islamic shrine that contains the Foundation Stone. This slab of rock is, in Orthodox Jewish belief, the place where G-d formed Adam, where Abraham offered up Isaac for sacrifice, and where Jacob dreamed about angels ascending and descending a ladder. It is thought to have been the location of the Ark of the Covenant in the First Temple, which, along with the Urim and Thummim, the high priest's divining objects (about which little is known for sure), disappeared after the first destruction.

It is also the rock from which Mohammad is said to have ascended to Heaven to confer with Allah, and is, thus, the third-holiest site in all of Islam.

And—talk about location, location, location—the Al-Aqsa Mosque is also part of this complex. This is the place to which Mohammad was flown from Mecca on the winged steed Buraq, around 621 CE, in what is known as the Night Journey. The mosque proper has been built, destroyed by multiple earthquakes, occupied, pillaged, and rebuilt many times.

How the construction of a Third Temple will be possible on a site so sacred to one and a half billion Muslims remains to be seen.

5

How to Obtain and Mount a Mezuzah

What is a *mezuzah?* It's that little object attached to the frames of the front doors of Jewish houses or apartments. Inside it is a tiny scroll on which is written a few prayers.

Okay, you know that. Let's just add these interesting facts:

✡ The word *mezuzah* is a transliteration of the Hebrew word for "doorpost." The commandment to have a *mezuzah* comes from Deuteronomy 6:9, in which G-d orders the Chosen People to commit fully to "these words, which I command thee this day." Thus: "And thou shalt write them upon the doorposts of thy house, and upon thy gates." If you really want to go all the way and comply strictly with Jewish law, you must put one on every doorframe in your home, not counting bathrooms and closets. Really.

✡ The scroll inside the *mezuzah* contains the Shema, the prayer from Deuteronomy 6:4–9 and 11:13–21 beginning "Hear, O Israel, the Lord is our God, the Lord is One." This may seem somewhat redundant—if He's "the Lord" then He is automatically "our God." It would be like saying, "Hear, O Israel, Doctor Sheldon Greenberg, my primary-care doctor, is my primary-care physician." But remember that, back then, members of most religions worshipped multiple gods. The Shema, then, is how Jews remind each other, and remind G-d, that we know that our god is the *only* god, and not a bunch of gods like the Egyptians had back then, with the Osiris and the Ra and the Thoth and the Ptah and whatnot.

✡ The scroll must be handwritten, or drawn, or calligraphed, or inscribed, or whatever the verb is, by a trained *mezuzzist*. No, that's not really a word. Actually the word is *sofer*—a trained Hebrew calligrapher.

Buying or Ordering the Mezuzah

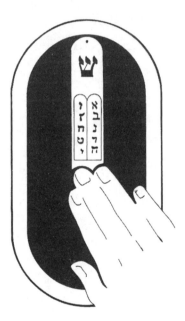

You would think that, in this day and age, obtaining a *mezuzah* would be as easy as typing *mezuzah* in the Google search field, clicking on the sites it provides (with names like mezuzah.com and mezuzahstore.com), and ordering one online, to be delivered to the very door on which you plan to mount it. And you would be right.

Or, of course, you can go to any synagogue or Judaica store and actually try one out before purchasing. As with everything from baby delivery to funerals, *mezuzot* (the plural) come in a wide range of prices, as well as an almost infinite range of materials, styles, and looks. As long as it contains a hand-drawn scroll of the Shema, it doesn't matter what the outer casing is.

Since it's the first thing people will see (if they see it) when they come to your home, be sure the *mezuzah* you display is an accurate embodiment of your style. If you have one.

Mounting the *Mezuzah*

According to Jewish law, the *mezuzah* should be mounted on the right side of the door (i.e., facing it as though entering the home), in the upper third of the frame. Fine.

Note, though, that if you live in the United States or, indeed, anywhere except Israel itself, in either a house or an apartment, *and are a renter*, you are required to mount the *mezuzah* within thirty days of move-in. If you live in Israel, whether you own or rent a house or an apartment, you are required to install the *mezuzah* immediately upon move-in.

You may affix the *mezuzah* to the doorpost with nails, screws, double-sided tape, or glue. *Halakha*, or combined Jewish religious and secular law, is silent as to whether you can use Krazy Glue, so go ahead; as everyone knows, you can do some crazy things with it. Although, frankly, gluing the *mezuzah* to the doorpost of thy house *would* be crazy, because it will make problematical your being able to remove it later if you have to move.

As to its orientation, make the *mezuzah* slant slightly toward the inside of the house, just to avoid arguments with all the Ashkenazi, Spanish, and Portuguese Jews you'll be having over. Some believe it should be mounted vertically, some horizontally. Slanting it toward the interior is a compromise.

In any case, slanting it also embodies the idea that G-d and the Torah are entering the home. So after you mount the *mezuzah*, clean up at least the living room.

The mezuzah is more than just a passive symbol of piety and dedication you display on a doorframe. It also provides a way to illustrate the differences in outlook between Orthodox, Conservative, and Reform Judaism.

A man scores a huge win in business, so to reward himself he buys a new Tesla. Then he starts to have pangs of guilt. Is it too much? Is it too extravagant? He decides to assuage these feelings by mounting a *mezuzah* on the car, but he isn't sure where to get the appropriate *mezuzah*.

He goes to an Orthodox rabbi and asks, "Reb, where can I get a *mezuzah* for my new Tesla?"

The rabbi frowns and says, "For what? What is this?"

"My new Tesla. It's an all-electric sports car."

The rabbi flies into a rage. "You want to desecrate a *mezuzah* by putting it on a car? Never!" And he kicks the man out of his office.

So the man goes to a Conservative rabbi and asks, "Rabbi, where can I get a *mezuzah* for my Tesla?"

"Your what?"

"Tesla. It's an all-electric sports car."

This rabbi, too, is upset. "I'm sorry, that is an entirely inappropriate use of a *mezuzah*. Please, don't waste my time."

The man has one option left, so he goes to speak to a Reform rabbi. He asks, "Rabbi, where can I get a *mezuzah* to put on my new Tesla?"

This rabbi says, "A Tesla?"

"Yes," the man says. "It's an all-electric sp—"

"Oh, I know what a Tesla is," the rabbi says. "But tell me—what is a *mezuzah*?"

6

LEARN TO EMBRACE *FIDDLER*

Want a fun, easy way to celebrate your Judaism without having to go to *shul*, fast, travel to Israel, or fork over money to the United Jewish Appeal? Make a nice brisket and have people over to screen the only American musical in history starring a man whose name is identical to a brand of tooth polish (i.e., Topol).

Fiddler on the Roof.

Universally referred to, by showbiz people and Jews, as *Fiddler*, this musical opened in 1964, with music by Jerry Bock and lyrics by Sheldon Harnick (*Fiorello!*), and book by Joseph Stein (*Zorba*). It starred Zero Mostel, whose beloved depiction of Tevye the Milkman prompted millions to ask, "What kind of a name is Zero? Is it Jewish for Zorro?" The first musical to run for more than three thousand performances on Broadway, it captured the hearts of Americans and Jews from all countries and of all faiths—

Okay, everybody older than twenty-one is familiar with *Fiddler*. The point is that revisiting it can do a lot to renew your flagging sense of Jewishness *even though it is just a Broadway musical.*

While you're at it, use your DVD player's remote control to search for and replay some of the musical numbers until you have them committed to memory. You don't have to learn all the songs, but you should at least be able to quote extensively from these:

- "Tradition"
- "If I Were a Rich Man"
- "Sunrise, Sunset"

You should also be able to hum and murmur a few key words incorrectly, from:

- "Matchmaker"
- "To Life"
- "Anatevka"

In addition, study the quotes from the show, below, and work them into your everyday conversation:

Man in Front: "'If I were a rich man . . .'"

Woman Beside Him: "Stop singing! We're not even Jewish!"

- "Tell me what you dreamed and I'll tell you what it meant."
- (in answer to a question) "I'll tell you. I don't know."
- "Right? Of course right!"
- "I realize, of course, that it's no shame to be poor." (Beat.) "But it's no great honor, either."

After fully immersing yourself (again, or for the first time) in *Fiddler*, find a production of it. It can be anywhere—at a college, a rep theater, a high school, a summer camp, whatever. Then make a big cultural deal out of dragging your children, nieces and nephews, or just random young people to it, as though sponsoring a pilgrimage to Mecca.

And don't let them try to get out of it by claiming they don't like musicals. It's their older siblings or people in their twenties who don't like musicals. Younger kids today have made *High School Musical* a huge, huge smash. They're ready.

7

How to Order Cantonese Food

Before there was Szechuan, with its jazzy hot peppers and liberal use of garlic and ginger; before there was Hunan, with its even hotter peppers and elaborate multistage preparations; before there was hoisin sauce and hot bean paste and fermented black beans . . . before Chinese food in the United States was synonymous with color and fire and zest, there was Cantonese.

Szechuan and Hunan are the Chinese foods of the culinarily sophisticated, over-assimilated American Jew. Cantonese, at least as it was served in the United States, was the Chinese of the post-WWII, suburban, less assimilated American Jew. It was particularly well suited to the delicate digestive systems of many Jews, whose taste for wild and crazy spicy things was vetoed by their touchy, sensitive stomachs.

Cantonese food has onions and bok choy and cornstarch and mild broth and bamboo shoots and water chestnuts and eggs and cornstarch and onions. There are noodles and soy sauce, to an extent. Yippee.

For excitement there's red-tinged roast pork, spare ribs, and scallions. And that's *it*. There were (and are) actual Cantonese versions of "Cantonese" dishes that made use of fermented beans and ginger and interesting and yummy whatnot, but American Cantonese was (and probably still is) doggedly bland—or, as food writers put it, "delicate." This, remember, was the Chinese food around which the stereotype developed that an hour after eating it you felt hungry again.

So let's bring it back! It's a delightful way to renew your allegiance to traditional Judaism: Dine on the dishes our parents or grandparents enjoyed when Mao was still in power, a "wok" was baby talk for a stone, and no one had ever heard of Hot and Sour Soup.

To help you make the transition between cuisines, we've created the chart below. Simply find the Szechuan or Hunan dish you're used to ordering, find its (approximate) Cantonese equivalent, and you're all set.

(Note: Do not make the mistake of thinking that Shrimp in Lobster Sauce, which seems to promise not one but two *trayf* [nonkosher] ingredients in a starring role, actually contains lobster. It doesn't. The reference is to the fermented black beans in the sauce, which is traditionally served with lobster. It should really be called Shrimp in What Is Normally a Sauce for Lobster, although it goes without saying that the American Cantonese version of that sauce doesn't have the black beans, either. To sum up: Shrimp in Lobster Sauce doesn't have lobster, and it doesn't have lobster sauce.)

Szechuan/Hunan-to-Cantonese Conversion Table

Szechuan or Hunan Dish	Approximate Cantonese Equivalent
Hot and Sour Soup	Wonton Soup
Wor Wonton Soup	Wonton Soup
Chicken and Corn Soup	Egg Drop Soup
Spring Rolls	Egg Rolls
Cold Noodles in Sesame Sauce	Pork-Fried Rice

(continued)

Szechuan or Hunan Dish	Approximate Cantonese Equivalent
General Tso's Chicken	Chicken Chow Mein
Chicken with Broccoli	Chicken Chow Mein
Chicken in Garlic Sauce	Chicken Chow Mein
Hunan Chicken	Chicken Chow Mein
Szechuan Chicken	Chicken Chow Mein
Cashew Chicken	Subgum Chicken Chow Mein
Kung Pao Chicken	Moo Goo Gai Pan
Chicken in Black Bean Sauce	Chicken Chow Mein
Sweet and Sour Chicken	Sweet and Sour Chicken
Orange Chicken	Chicken Chow Mein
Beef with Broccoli	Beef Chow Mein
Mongolian Beef	Beef Chow Mein
Dry-Fried Beef	Beef Chow Mein
Beef with Oyster Sauce	Beef Chow Mein
Orange Beef	Beef Chow Mein
Moo Shu Pork	Cantonese Steamed Pork
Twice-Cooked Pork	Once-Cooked Pork (Pork Char Siu)
Sweet and Sour Pork	Sweet and Sour Pork
Ginger shrimp	Shrimp in Lobster Sauce
Hunan Shrimp	Shrimp in Lobster Sauce
Spicy Southern Prawns	Shrimp in Lobster Sauce
Shrimp in Black Bean Sauce	Shrimp in Lobster Sauce
Triple-Treasure Crispy Emerald Empress's Golden Happy-Go-Lucky Spicy Delight	Shrimp in Lobster Sauce

A Joke About Pork

Speaking of pork, we are reminded in this context of the following story: A rabbi acquired a real craving for pork, but was embarrassed to be seen eating it by any of his congregation. So he drove a hundred miles out of the community and found a Chinese restaurant he was sure his congregants never frequented. He ordered the most lavishly pork-based item on the menu: an entire roasted suckling pig. When it was brought to the table he was pleased to note that it had, in its mouth, the traditional apple. But just as he was about to dig in, he sensed some-one standing behind him, and heard a familiar voice saying, "Rabbi—?"

It was Mrs. Lefkowitz, from the Sisterhood. The rabbi greeted her, and then gestured indignantly toward the roast pig and said, "Do you believe it? I ordered an apple, and *this* is how it came."

8

USE THE JEWISH CALENDAR!

t happens all the time. Someone says, "You know, I was wondering— in 2011, is Halloween on the third or fourth of Cheshvan?"

You might not know. But it doesn't have to be that way. With a little study, you can be the one to pipe up, "Actually, it's on the third of Cheshvan. And a week later, on the tenth of Cheshvan, is the last day of National Fig Week."

Impressive? You bet. The Jewish calendar offers an especially potent tool for reconnecting with your tribal roots. Why settle for the puny year 2010, when you can place dates in a context almost three times larger? Imagine how robustly Jewish you'll feel when someone asks, "Hey, what are you doing on Lag B'Omer in 2012?" and you say, "You mean on the eighteenth of Iyar in the year 5772? Let me check . . ."

There's probably a smart-phone app for converting dates from the Gregorian to the Jewish calendar—in fact there are probably thirty of them—but in case there aren't any, or you're one of those unfortunates who has to suffer with a dumb phone, the fundamentals are pretty straightforward.

The Gregorian calendar is solar, and the Jewish is lunar. There's an eleven-day difference between the two, which means that the Jewish calendar, if left uncorrected, would creep out of sync not only with the world's Gregorian calendar, but with its own agricultural and holiday requirements. That's why, over a nineteen-year cycle of 235 lunar months, certain years receive an intercalary thirteenth month. This takes place every two or three years, or seven times per nineteen years. Clear? Never mind.

For simplicity's sake, just remember that the Jewish calendar year consists of twelve months, except for the third, sixth, eighth, eleventh, fourteenth, seventeenth, and nineteenth years in each nineteen-year cycle, in which it contains thirteen months. The names of the months, and the number of days each has, are as follows:

Name of Month	Number of Days
1. Nisan	30
2. Iyar	29
3. Sivan	30
4. Tamuz	29
5. Av	30
6. Elul	29
7. Tishrei	30
8. Cheshvan	29 or 30
9. Kislev	30 or 29
10. Tevet	29
11. Shevat	30
12. Adar I (leap years only)	30
13. Adar (or Adar II in leap years)	29

To include in this table a column for which Gregorian calendar month is most often associated with which Jewish calendar month would be too complicated. Just bear in mind that Cheshvan and Kislev are left flexible so that certain holy days don't fall on prohibited days. Adar II (called just plain Adar in non–leap years) is the "leap month" added every three years or so.

When a Jew says, "I'm so *feshtoodled* [confused, disoriented] I don't know what day it is," now you know why.

To make things even more interesting, the days of the week have no proper names, except for Shabbat. The other six are simply designated by their number (First Day, Second Day, etc.). And each day begins, as you may know, at sundown, when three second-magnitude stars are just visible, and ends just prior to sundown twenty-four hours (more or less) later. In other words, each day begins at night, because that's how the Book of Genesis defined Creation's first days.

Each new month begins when the crescent of the new moon appears—an event that used to be announced by official observers, but that is now determined by mathematical calculation.

Oh, and one more detail: Rosh Hashanah (Head of the Year, the Jewish New Year) marks the start of the religious year, and falls on the

"All right, I know this. 'Thirty days has Nisan, Sivan, Av, Tishrei, Cheshvan . . . and Tevet'? No, wait. Okay. 'Thirty days . . . '"

first of Tishrei. But check that table above—the calendar designates the month of Nisan, in spring, as the start of the "civil year."

The solar calendar is for wimps. It takes a Real Jew to be able to pinpoint dates in a lunar year.

Knowing the Jewish date of some stranger's birthday five years from now could be just the sort of show-offy, incomprehensible bar-bet trick likely to win you both the wager *and* a punch in the nose. A profitable monetary transaction plus brutal physical oppression: Nothing's more Jewish than that.

9

USE THE BIBLE TO TELL IF
YOUR WIFE IS UNFAITHFUL

A ny man, Jew or non, can hire a stranger to spy on his wife. It takes a Real Jew, or someone aspiring to be one, to test his wife's fidelity by applying a technique that goes all the way back to the Book of Numbers—which, by the way, is (unlike many books) *still in print*.

And this, from a book that first came out in its present form in the Fifth Century BCE. That's 2,500 years of proven success (or at least not proven failure) at detecting cheating wives. Why *wouldn't* you use the following classic method?

Compassionate-looking rabbi presents possibly unfaithful wife with water infused with dust from tabernacle.

How to Tell if Your Wife Is Being Unfaithful

1. Take your wife to "the priest." Since in the modern era the word "priest" has acquired certain non-Jewish connotations, the word "rabbi" will be used henceforth.

2. When you go, bring a tenth of an ephah of barley flour. (An ephah is equal to a tenth of a homer, or about one bushel. So just bring about one one-hundredth of a homer. You do know what a homer is, right? Good. Be sure not to pour oil on it or put incense on it.)

3. The rabbi will usher your wife to stand before the Lord. Then he will take some holy water in a clay jar and put some dust from the tabernacle (i.e., the synagogue) floor into it.

4. The rabbi will loosen your wife's hair and place in her hands the barley flour as he holds the jar of water. He will place her "under oath."

5. Then he will intone something to the effect of, "If you have been faithful, may this bitter water not harm you. But if you have committed adultery and defiled yourself by sleeping with a man who is not your husband, may the Lord cause your people to curse and denounce you"—"your people," in this case, doesn't mean your assistants and personal shopper and the rest of your entourage, but your family—"and may this water enter your body and cause your abdomen to swell and your thigh to waste away." Granted, some women can't wait for at least some of *both* of their thighs to waste away, but we think this process will not be what they have in mind.

6. Your wife is then to say, "Amen. So be it." Be sure, when she says this, that she doesn't mean, "Yes, please! I can't wait to have thinner thighs." Be sure she understands the gravity of the situation.

7. The rabbi will then write this curse on a scroll and wash it off in the water. He will give the jar to your wife and have her drink the water while he takes the barley flour from her.

8. He will then wave the barley flour before the Lord, and burn some of it at the altar. Since most altars in modern synagogues are not equipped for burnt sacrifices, he can just dribble some onto a burning candle.

9. Your wife will drink all the bitter water. Then the waiting begins.

10. If she has been faithful, then she will suffer no ill effects from the water. She'll be cleared, found not guilty, and allowed to go on her way. The Torah says she "will be able to have children," although she'll also be able to resume doing the things that made you suspicious of her in the first place.

11. If, however, she *is* guilty of adultery, her abdomen will swell and her thigh will waste away. We don't know how long this will take, so give it a day or so. If her belly gets big and her thigh(s?) shrinks and shrivels, she will be accursed among your and her people, not to mention among you. Presumably this will mean you are either free to divorce her, to "save" it as ammunition for future arguments, or to go have a fling of your own.

And that's all there is to it. It's easy and fast, and costs significantly less than hiring a licensed gumshoe. What's more, you not only get to determine whether or not she's been running around, but you get to embrace and reaffirm your Jewishness. Win-win!

10
HOW AND WHY TO MAKE CHOPPED LIVER

ctually the title is backward. The first matter to address is: Why? Why should you eat chopped liver?

One answer is that chopped liver is an iconic Jewish food. Sure, so is chicken soup with matzoh balls—but who cares? They're not disgusting enough. The whole point of an ethnic or national food icon is that it be a) exclusively identified with the ethnic or national group in question; b) famous enough to be known about by "outsiders"; and c) seemingly—or actually—repellent.

Examples abound. Is anything more Scottish, or Scot, or Scotch, than haggis? Or more gross? It begins with a sheep's heart, liver, and lungs chopped and stuffed into the animal's stomach along with suet and oatmeal. It's all downhill from there. Certainly there are non-offputting examples of French food (French fries, French toast, etc.), but it's foie gras (which, in fact, is French for "chopped liver") that stands as the exemplar of that nation's culinary heritage. And how do you go about making that? Glad you asked: You shove corn down the gullet of a goose and then, eventually, eat its liver. And who can forget, no matter how hard they try, *menudo*, a Mexican tripe soup, which includes honeycomb tripe, beef feet, and tendons—oh, and there's a Filipino version that includes (don't blame us; we're just the messengers) *raisins*; lutefisk from Scandinavia—whitefish soaked in water and lye; and a Taiwanese dish with a charming name somewhat evocative of a naughty cartoon character: stinky tofu. Nauseating, all, and all proud embodiments of their respective national characters.

But there is another reason chopped liver is important: its dual nature.

Chopped liver occupies the paradoxical place in Jewish culture as something both highly cherished *and* synonymous with irrelevance. Jews talk about chopped liver as though it were the apex of the Eastern European and Russian culinary tradition. If a deli doesn't feature this dish, the place is dismissed as being as inauthentic and homogenized as a slice of pizza at Disneyland. And yet it is quite common to hear the very people who praise and fetishize chopped liver turn around and dis it completely.

To better understand this, and thus to better restore your original, unassimilated Jewishness, find another person and practice the following dialogue:

> **You:** Mmm, chopped liver. It's my favorite.
> **Other Person:** So what if it's your favorite? Who cares what you like?
> **You:** What am I, chopped liver?

(You can tell that the preceding dialogue is Jewish because 60 percent of it consists of rhetorical questions.)

It is possible that a nontrivial number of young Jewish boys and girls have been made schizophrenic by the confusion engendered by this dual meaning. If so, they should have a little chopped liver. It's delicious! In fact, chopped liver is "a delicacy," which is a haute cuisine term meaning "tasty, as long as you don't know what it really is."

Thus, anyone seeking to upgrade his or her Jewishness should learn to love chopped liver and, if they already love it, to make it.

No doubt there are some readers thinking, "How hard can it be to make chopped liver? You take some liver, and you chop it!" If only cooking, and life itself, were that easy. Still, it's not really difficult.

The main question that confronts one when making chopped liver is: chicken liver or calf liver? There are recipes using either but most people probably tend to default to chicken. Calf liver, when broiled, can have that rubbery-leathery firmness that makes your skin crawl, whereas chicken liver—although no less disgusting in its raw state than calf's—can cook up to be rather tender and appealing.

The liver(s) is/are sautéed—in chicken fat, if you really mean it—or broiled. You chop/process/etc. onions, and maybe mushrooms. You could deglaze the pan with Madeira or sherry. You chop/process the liver and add chopped hard-boiled eggs, thyme, parsley, whatever. Toss it all together, season, chill. Serve on crackers, matzoh, that sort of thing.

It has an off-putting smell and a color similar to that of window putty, and can be sort of grainy and mushy in the mouth, but still: It's not bad. And *tres* Jewish. Try it!

"Is something wrong, darling? You hardly touched your chopped liver."

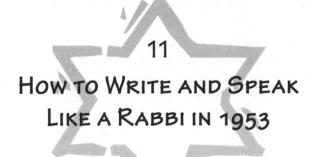

11

HOW TO WRITE AND SPEAK
LIKE A RABBI IN 1953

"Thank you, Principal Smith. It is a particular pleasure for
me to address this year's graduating class of fine middle
school ninth-graders, and the occasion puts me in mind
of an amusing comment made by the great sage Maimonides in the late twelfth century . . ."

In your quest to return to your traditional Jewish roots, you can follow every suggestion in this book and still, somehow, come up short.
How is this possible? Because mere behavior isn't enough. Simply
doing new (i.e., old) things won't be sufficient to transform you as a
person.

For that, you need to make alterations to your very mind. To become the Jew you used to be, or that you would have been if only you had been born in the nineteenth century, you need to change not only what you do, but how you think and express yourself.

That's why we suggest learning to write—and, ideally, think—like one of those polysyllabic, droning rabbis people used to encounter at Bar Mitzvahs during the 1950s and early '60s. These men (and they were men only, then) possessed both infinite patience and an enormous respect for the turgidly written and monotonously intoned word. The traditional Jewish reverence for ideas, for books, for commentary and commentary on the commentary and commentary on the commentary on the commentary . . .

Learn to write and speak like those rabbis, and you'll not only feel like a scholar and a sage, but you'll be treated like one, too. Simply follow these simple, followable steps:

1. **Take your time.** Jews have been debating and lecturing and discussing and elaborating for 5,700 years. "Talmudic" is a synonym for hairsplitting, endlessly refined excurses. Your taking ten or fifteen minutes to say something a normal person can say in twenty seconds isn't going to do any harm, at this point.

2. **Lovingly dwell on and thoroughly lay out every thought, no matter how potentially small, tangential, or obvious.** For example, instead of saying, "Everyone loves hot dogs," say, "It is an indisputable fact, confirmable through even the most cursory examination of popular literature as well as via consultation with our own personal experience and through inquiries directed at friends and loved ones, that the preponderance of people in society today are fond, if not actually enamored of, the kinds of sausages most often designated—interestingly by both the cultured 'elite' and by the so-called 'hoi polloi'—as 'hot dogs.'"

3. **Concision, pace, momentum, and an appealing rhythm are the enemies of the rabbinic style.** If you find yourself employing any of these rhetorical techniques, walk away and take a nap. When you wake up, strive for entangled clauses, infinitely recursive

qualifications, and a kind of treadmill-like laboriousness. Your goal should be something that feels, to the listener or the reader, like it must be going somewhere worthwhile, and yet is inevitably disappointing when it arrives. If it ever does arrive.

For example, instead of writing, "Call me Ishmael," write, "My name, insofar as it will prove germane to the present narrative, and especially considering the exigencies of the first-person voice, the use of which almost, if not entirely, mitigates against the usage of the narrator's name, usually requiring nothing more than its substitution by 'I' or 'me' and thus rendering its knowledge not only superfluous to the reader, but arguably downright confusing, is, for purposes of completeness, the need for which is, admittedly, itself open to question, Ishmael."

4. Pretend to have a sense of humor. In speaking or writing in a formal context, start with a joke or with a "humorous anecdote" recounting something that really happened. Whether you're giving a talk to a professional group, addressing a civic meeting, or just offering a toast at a wedding, opening with a "laugh" is a great way to lead in to the deeply serious material to follow.

Your joke or anecdote should go on at length and thus seem like it's going to end in a revelation about the human condition. For example: "It is wonderful to see you all here for this wonderful occasion. And, you know, it puts me in mind of something that I witnessed a few years ago at a baseball game. The [insert home team] were playing the [insert rival team], and in between the top and the bottom of the third inning, while the visiting team had just taken the field and was warming up, suddenly a fellow jumped out of the stands and ran to home plate, and from there ran to first base, and all around the bases while several security officers tried to detain him. And he managed to make it all the way around third base and back to home plate before he was captured. As they were leading him off the field, he suddenly tore his shirt off and waved it at the crowd. And the man beside me commented, 'It's a good thing he wasn't a woman!'"

As in this example, your joke or anecdote should in no way be the least bit funny. But it should end with what is obviously (or is obviously supposed to be) a punch line in order to cue a wry chuckle of recognition from whomever is still awake listening to you or reading you. Don't be fooled, however; this chuckle will not indicate that you've "killed." It will just be the audience's way of attempting to retain consciousness. And that's all you ask.

5. Always be exhausted. If not physically, then emotionally or morally. This attitude will make telling your joke or humorous anecdote seem particularly thoughtful and noble, as though you are expending energy and merriment you really can't afford strictly to provide your audience with a little pleasure. It will also make people who don't find the joke funny or the anecdote humorous feel ashamed of themselves, which will soften them up and make them all the more receptive to your subsequent observations.

6. Use fancy words, i.e., employ an elaborate and heightened vocabulary. As the examples above illustrate, using words of three or more syllables, as often as possible and certainly more than necessary, is essential to convey not only your seriousness, but the respect you have for civilized discourse, for accurate communication, for thoroughgoing discussion, for sophisticated ideas, and for just about everything except the listener or reader.

7. Invert ordinary sentence construction. Nothing says "deep, meaningful thinking" like turning sentences around. For example, instead of saying, "There are many different kinds of hubcaps at a junkyard," say, "Many and varied are the varieties of hubcaps to be found at a junkyard." Don't say, "Tom drove to Phoenix to pick up the breakfront." Rather, say, "To Phoenix drove Tom, there to pick up the breakfront."

The idea isn't necessarily to talk or write like Yoda (although he *is* the rabbi of the Star Wars movies), but to imbue what you're saying with a glow of antique grandeur, no matter how boring or obvious it is. *Especially* if it's boring or obvious.

12

HOW TO PUT YOUR YARMULKE ON
SO IT STAYS ON

Men! What do you do if you want to reconnect with your Jewishness? That's right, you go to Jewish ritual events. You attend a *seder*. You take part in post–Yom Kippur breaking-of-the-fast. Maybe, alas, you go to a funeral. Perhaps you even go to synagogue.

At each of these, someone hands around *yarmulkes*, so you put one on but, after a few moments of refreshing piety, you inevitably find yourself wondering: "Why does my *yarmulke* keep falling off?"

There are many possible reasons. Perhaps you have, literally, a *Yiddishe kopf*, i.e., a "Jewish head." This colloquial expression means "thinks like a Jew" (e.g., "Scorsese? Catholic, obviously. But in some ways, has a *Yiddishe kopf*."). In your case, though, your actual, physiological head may be so profoundly of Jewish descent that you're either balding, with no even terrain for the garment to hang on to, or you sport a "Jewfro," the big, lush, springy head of hair off of which skullcaps bounce like kids on a trampoline.

Maybe the *yarmulke* you're wearing is made of a particularly slippery satin. Or, even if it's made of rugged, head-grabbing suede, it's too small to obtain sufficient purchase on the skull.

Or maybe you're not bald *enough*. Out of two entirely bald individuals, one says keeping a *kippah* on is no problem whatsoever, while the other reports good luck with suede (although he did express frustration with satin/polyester).

Then again, it could be that you're just not wearing it right, slapping it down on the wrong cranial location.

Whatever the cause, it's annoying to constantly feel that slippage, to sense the little Frisbee of fabric sliding off, and to have to bend over and retrieve it and reposition it. And then sit stiffly upright, not moving, like an android, hoping for the best.

Do not despair. There are several strategies for keeping the *kippah* on your *keppie*. Here they are in ascending order of practicality.

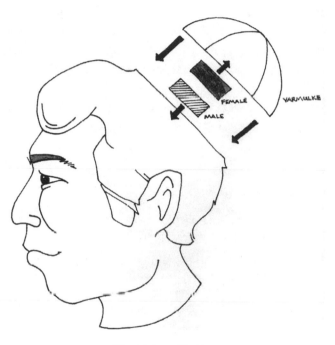

The Velcro Option

1. Velcro. Cut about a square inch each of the two halves (the bristly, or "male," half and the loop, or "female," half) of a sheet of Velcro. Cut two pieces, about ¾ inch each, of two-sided tape, or cut two 1½-inch strips of ordinary masking tape and bend each into a ring and tape it to itself with the sticky side out. Attach one piece of the double-sided tape or the looped masking tape to the crown of your head. Affix the "male" piece of Velcro to it. Attach the other piece of tape to the *yarmulke* at the center of its underside and affix the "female" piece of Velcro to that. Then, to wear the *yarmulke,* simply position it on your head so the Velcro pads meet. Press gently but firmly. The *kippah* will remain in place until you pry it off. Of course, removing the tape from your head—like ripping a Band-Aid off a wound—will require great courage and the possible loss of a few hairs. But it's worth it.

2. Party hat elastic. We recommend a crocheted *kippah* for this technique; otherwise, you'll have to cut or poke two small holes at opposite positions (at, for example, 3:00 and 9:00) on the *kippah.* Take the elastic band off a party hat (each end of which is attached to a small sticklike endpiece), insert the endpieces through the holes in the *kippah,* and wear the elastic under the chin, like a football or army helmet (or a party hat). It's not elegant, but it works.

3. String. See No. 2, above. If party hat elastic is unavailable, use ordinary string or twine. It will look crude and unfinished, and in fact silly, but it, too, will work.

4. Bobby pin or hair clip. The above two strategies will work regardless of how much hair you have. This one works only if you have hair to clip onto. A bobby pin is more discreet but harder to affix. A spring-loaded hair clip is more blatant but easier to put on and take off.

13

HOW TO BE PASSIVE-AGGRESSIVE, IF THAT'S WHAT YOU INSIST ON CALLING IT

You might be thinking, "Seriously? Passive-aggressive? I thought the Jewish stereotype in the classic era of the twentieth century, when *menschen* were *menschen*, was the *opposite* of passive-aggressive. I thought Jews were supposedly pushy."

There are two theories about the origins of Jewish passive-aggressiveness. Both begin with "being pushy."

First, pushiness is not so much a Jewish trait as it is a merchant's trait. It's a style assumed by salesmen (and -women) eager to buy and sell and wheel and deal. Jews embodied this in America, but so did many other ethnic groups. The stereotype of the (lower- and middle-class) "pushy Jew" may have been the disdainful creation of (upper-class) Gentiles, among whom commercial transactions were conducted with clubby chitchat, old-boy courtesy, and ritualistic politesse.

Pushy was how some classes got ahead. Genteel was how other classes stayed ahead.

The second theory—and remember, evolution itself is a "theory," and look at how authoritative that is—is that Jews, in an effort to assimilate and to "be American," consciously rejected pushiness. But they discovered that, in so doing, they still needed a way to get what they wanted, if not in business then socially. So they invented being passive-aggressive, which, in its subtlety and indirectness, is a kind of Zen Judaism.

Still, you can go pushy. You can learn to come off as a pugnacious go-getter, a fast-talking, hard-bargaining guy or gal, the kind of person who's always putting his or her cards on the table even when there's no table and there aren't any cards. You may get some positive results, but you won't feel more in touch with your inner Jew. You'll feel in touch with your inner hustler.

"But wait!" some will say. "What you just described—isn't that *hondling*? For which this book has an entire entry?"

Yes, it is. But *hondling* is an aggressive-aggressive way of conducting

"No, that's all right, I don't really need any water. You get some for yourself. You're young, you're very busy. I'll be fine."

commercial transactions in the marketplace, even if that "marketplace" is someone's yard sale. For dealing with friends, family, lovers, and others in situations in which money is not an issue, we suggest you learn to be *passive*-aggressive in the classic manner of the Jewish mothers of yesteryear. These were the women who could manipulate you into doing what they wanted by a) making you think that it was your idea, or b) making you feel guilty, not only for not doing it, but for not *wanting* to do it.

The dividends and benefits of this technique of persuasion can hardly be overstated. Not only do you get what you want from the other person, but you seem to do so innocently, honestly, and without being bossy and horrible. You're not coercing them; *they're coercing themselves.* Thus, you not only manipulate them into doing your bidding, but you can disclaim all responsibility afterward if things go wrong.

It sounds like a combination of magic and hypnosis—and it is. But it's not that hard to learn. Study the following Basic Principles of Passive-Aggressiveness and see how easy it can be. Or don't, if that's what you really want.

Basic Principles of Passive-Aggressiveness

1. Never affirmatively say that you want thing X. Instead, drop hints and pretend to be flustered and shy. Say "well" a lot to indicate your (fake) reluctance to even bring it up.

Example:

Other Person: What's wrong?
You: Nothing. . . .
Other Person: No, really.
You: Well . . . it's just . . . Didn't you say we were going to see that new Jennifer Aniston movie tonight?
Other Person: I did?
You: Well, you said *something.*
Other Person: Why? Is that what you want to do?

2. Once the other party guesses (or is told) what X is and asks if you want it, deny it. This is essential. The last thing you want to reveal, when you want something, is that you want something. The other person, sensing you're not being entirely forthcoming, will try to draw you out. Resist this and hint that maybe the other person is being just a bit of a bully—which is all the more wounding because you've been thinking about what the other person wants all along.

Example:

You: Me? Oh, no! I don't care. . . .
Other Person: Well, I mean, you brought it up.
You: I didn't bring it up. I was just thinking about *you*. . . .

3. Now, having told the other person what he or she wants, execute the Passive-Aggressive Switcheroo and tell them, or imply, they want exactly the opposite. Be sure to make their position sound as perverse, unpleasant, painful, boring, etc., as possible, and hint—broadly—that they're causing you to suffer, *and that you accept that.*

Example:

You (cont'd.): . . . although if you want to just forget it and stay home, I guess I can find some other way to see it. It's all right. . . .

4. When the other person tries to assuage the suffering they have caused, don't buy it. Refuse their offer of sympathy or help. Be brave in your selflessness.

Example:

Other Person: No, it's fine. We can go see it if you really want to.
You: Look, I don't care. I'll be fine. Whatever you want to do is okay with me.

NOTE: The sentence "Whatever you want to do is okay with me" is the most important tool in the passive-aggressive's kit. It has the combined power of "Open, sesame" and "There's no place like home." It's both apparently deferential (passive), but in context highly manipulative (aggressive). Use it with care. But use it.

5. At this critical moment, plant in the other person's consciousness the notion that the topic under discussion was his or her idea all along.
Example:

You: I just thought you said you wanted to see it. Which is fine with me.

6. At this point, you are not only locating your desire for X in the other person, but you are also selflessly agreeing to give the other person "their wish." Unless they are extremely argumentative (or extremely passive-aggressive), they will be so confused, they will believe it *was* their idea and insist on carrying it out. Or, they'll be so pissy and irritated for reasons they can't quite identify, they'll try to close out the conversation by agreeing to X. Make one final, token offer of accommodation, but don't push it. "Give in" happily, but not too happily.
Example:

Other Person: All right, whatever. Let's go see it.
You: Are you sure?
Other Person: Yes! Let's just go. Get your coat
You: You got it!

(Note "you got it." It concludes the process with a final reminder that this was the other person's idea, or at least that you thought it was, or at least you want the other person to think that you thought it was.)
You might wonder, "Why go through this whole elaborate and vaguely abusive bit of manipulation? Why not just say, 'Hey, I want to see the new Jennifer Aniston movie'?"
The answer is simple: Because if the other person says no, you're left with either disappointment or an argument.

Why take the chance? Isn't it better to brainwash someone into thinking they want what you want than to run the risk of someone, or everyone, expressing real emotions such as anger or exasperation? Our mothers and grandmothers thought so, and look at how Jewish they are!

14

THE MAJOR HOLIDAYS

Remember Jewish holidays—days when you, as a Jewish child, had to stay home from school and "celebrate" (by enduring at least a morning of mind-crushing synagogue tedium, followed by whatever kind of afternoon activity your parents permitted, given that it was a holiday), while your non-Jewish or nonobservant friends got to go to school and, because so many people were absent, probably just mess around and have fun?

One of the benefits of enduring childhood to make it to adulthood is you don't have to go to *shul* all morning just because it's Rosh Hashanah or Yom Kippur. In some cases, of course, you *can't*: Not every employer (or profession) allows you to skip work to attend services. But even if you like your job less than you liked school, would you if you could?

The major holidays offer a good

opportunity, or pretext or excuse, to attend a service to remind yourself what they were (and still are) all about. In the case of the High Holy Days (Rosh Hashanah and Yom Kippur) it's a mixed blessing. The good news is, the crowd will be at its maximum in terms of size and ardor; the bad news is that most synagogues charge money for tickets (it's one of their few sure-thing offerings), and these can run into the triple digits.

Still, there are Broadway shows that cost more and leave you feeling worse. And, as though attending a classic musical or opera or operetta, you'll recognize many of the key moments as they arrive and find yourself able to sing along with the showstoppers.

Here are the major Jewish holidays. All begin at sundown of the night before the designated day; those evening services are usually shorter and less important than the ones that follow the morning after.

Rosh Hashanah

It literally means "Head of the Year," but it falls on the first day of the seventh, not first, month of the Jewish calendar. It's considered the start of the civil year, i.e., the first of the year for people, animals, and contracts. To the devout it is the second holiest day of the year, after Yom Kippur.

Its origin goes back to—of all places—Babylonia. On that day of the year, the Babylonians celebrated a Day of Judgment, which they considered to be their New Year. The earliest names for Rosh Hashanah were Yom ha-Zikaron (Day of Remembrance) and Yom ha-Din (Day of Judgment)—both Babylonian concepts, referring to the assembly of their various deities in the great Temple of Marduk. Thus gathered, these gods would "renew" the world, remembering each man's and nation's deeds and judging them accordingly. The Jews, surrounded and permeated by this influence, began to observe a similar day on which G-d would evaluate men and women and determine their fate. (The first mention of "Rosh Hashanah" per se doesn't occur until the second century CE in the Mishnah, the code of the Oral Tradition.)

Thus, the Christian idea of the Last Judgment derives from the Jews, who derive it from Babylonian polytheism. Go know.

Rosh Hashanah is, in fact, merely the start of the Days of Awe, a ten-day period during which all men and women are to scrutinize their behavior over the previous year and make amends. The *shofar* is blown as a clarion call to "wake up" the sleeping awareness of the individual and spur him or her to repentance.

Meanwhile, a switcheroo was performed on the original Babylonian formula. The Day of Remembrance is not G-d's day to remember man; it's man's day to remember G-d, and to seek forgiveness for his human, mortal shortcomings.

Yom Kippur

Yom Kippur is the Day of Atonement, and there are those who believe the Hebrew word *kippur* derives from the Babylonian term meaning "to purge" or "to wipe out." Again with the polytheistic influences: Babylonians and Canaanites, like all peoples of the Assyrian-Babylonian civilization, believed in the necessity to propitiate the gods by making a collective atonement for human sins. How else to assure the safety of their flocks and herds, and the abundance of their corn?

The Jews, a morally self-conscious people, adopted this notion of collective guilt and collective redemption. In Biblical times, Yom Kippur was the day when atonement for the community was effected by the killing of two goats. The first was sacrificed as a sin-offering on the altar in the normal fashion. The second, however, had ceremonially bestowed upon it the sins of all the people. Then, to appease the evil demon Azazel, who infested the wilderness, this "scapegoat" was led up to a high bluff and thrown over it to its death, which was followed by a general rejoicing.

We don't do that anymore (where, as usual, "anymore" means "since 70 CE, when the Destruction of the Temple robbed us of a place in which to make animal sacrifices"). At least, we don't do it with goats. A small (and dwindling) minority of the Orthodox still perform a similar rite over a rooster or a hen, which is then ritually slaughtered in accordance with kosher regulations.

Goats aside, Yom Kippur is the day when G-d notes our behavior over the past year and our repentance, or lack thereof, since Rosh Hasha-nah, and either does or does not inscribe our name in the Book of Life for another year. Fasting, from sundown the night before to sundown of this day, seems the least one can do to mark the solemnity of the occasion.

You can also, if you want to go all the way, attend services the night before, where the *chazzan* (cantor) will sing the prayer Kol Nidre (All Vows) not once, not twice, but three times—like they used to do it back in the sixth or seventh century. It is the most solemn and, to many, the most moving of all Jewish prayers. And not just to Jews: Beethoven used a melodic excerpt of it in the eight opening bars of his "Quartet in C Sharp Minor."

Passover

This is probably the most beloved of the holidays (*pace* the *kinder* [the children], who, at least in the United States, probably prefer Chanu-kah), because it celebrates a liberation and offers an occasion for every household to host and direct its own mini-service, to which non-Jews are enthusiastically welcomed.

Officially, of course, Passover (from the Hebrew *pesach*, to pass over or spare) commemorates the Exodus from Egypt and the emancipation from slavery. Its poignancy links the Exodus, the Diaspora after the Second Temple's destruction, and the general state of oppression and humiliation suffered by Jews in an increasingly Christian world over the past two millennia. The subtext, to the extent that Jews, post-Diaspora, are scattered all over the world and subjects of maltreatment, is that we are *still* "slaves."

But how is it that this event—and Easter—just happened to fall in the month when (at least in the northern hemisphere) spring has finally taken hold? Coincidence?

Until the end of the First Temple period (c. 600 BCE), "Passover" combined two holidays: the Festival of Abib ("greening," or "spring") and the Festival of Matzot (plural of "matzoh," meaning "unleavened bread"). The former was a typical springtime revel, until such license was ended by no-fun scribes like Ezra and Nehemiah in the middle of the fifth century BCE. Abib was a seasonal harvest festival to propitiate the Deity in the hopes of good future crops. Somehow it got combined with the Festival of Unleavened Bread, celebrated in accordance with Exodus 23:15 (*The feast of unleavened bread shalt thou keep; seven days shalt thou eat unleavened, as I commanded thee, at the time appointed in the month of Abib* [i.e., in the month of spring], *for in it thou camest out of Egypt*).

Authorities differ as to whether the Feast of Unleavened Bread predated the Exodus, and was combined with an observance of it, or whether Passover *is* the Feast of Unleavened Bread. Leviticus 23:5 is ambiguous:

> *In the first month, on the fourteenth day of the month between the two evenings is the LORD's Passover. And on the fifteenth day of the same month is the feast of unleavened bread unto the LORD; seven days ye shall eat unleavened bread.*

In any case, there is unleavened bread—matzoh—and a ceremony held in the home, as first promulgated by the patriarch Rabban Gamaliel in the late first century. The *seder* (order) is the ceremonial meal, narrated and directed by the Haggadah (a "telling" or "tale"), a booklet that leads the assembled in a narrative of the Exodus, a series of prayers, and a commemorative discussion of the *Seder* Plate.

On this are displayed a roast shank bone of a lamb (a prime symbol of spring, and the animal whose blood, painted on the Jewish doorframes, alerted the Angel of Death to "pass over" as he went about slaying the first-born of the Egyptians); a roasted egg (a symbol of resurrection and immortality); some bitter herbs (e.g., horseradish, aka "Jewish cocaine"); a green vegetable (parsley); and *charoset*, a mixture of ground apples, raisins, almonds, cinnamon, and wine, to symbolize the mortar the Jewish slaves had been forced to make.

There are fun, or at least cute, rituals, including the asking, by the youngest child who can do it, of the Four Questions, which some say aren't questions at all, but exclamations—not "How is this night different from all other nights?" but, rather, "How different this night is from all other nights!" and so on.

There is also a cup of wine left untouched—ostensibly for Elijah, the prophet, should he happen to show up, although the custom of having a child open the door for him probably had its origin in the less fanciful need, in the Middle Ages, to show suspicious Christians that, inside, the Jews were in fact not murdering Gentile babies and using their blood for matzoh, but were simply having a ceremonial dinner.

There are many more rituals and customs:

Four "cups" of wine are drunk throughout the ceremony, each preceded by the traditional blessing. Whether participants restrict this to four sips or four entire goblets, or something in between, is a matter of house rules.

An adult hides a part of one of the three ceremonial pieces of matzoh, which is declared the *afikomin*, the "dessert" matzoh. Then the kids search for it, and whoever finds it holds it for a (reasonable) cash ransom, because without it, the *seder* cannot be completed.

At the end of the meal the assembled often sing the folk song "*Chad Gadya*" ("One Kid"), the Jewish version of "The House That Jack Built" ("The fire came, and burned the stick, that beat the dog, that bit the cat, that ate the goat/Which my father bought for two *zuzim* . . . ").

The entire event usually ends with the benediction "Next year in Jerusalem." All that, plus a recitation of the Ten Plagues that befell the Egyptians (blood . . . locusts . . .), the parting of the Red Sea, and a triumphant liberation: Even if you don't particularly "feel" celebrations like Simchat Torah or Purim, it's hard to resist Passover.

Chanukah

Some say this shouldn't be on this list, since Chanukah is a minor holiday and not that big a deal in Israel. But, to the extent that it's grown in significance in the United States—where, surrounded by Christmas gift-giving, Jews have obtained license to engage in gift-giving of their own—it shows exactly how "sacred" holidays can be influenced and shaped by other cultures. And it celebrates a triumph second only to that of Passover in significance, and even better than Passover as a tale not of departure but of military triumph.

In Judea (the southern part of Israel, now divided between Israel and the West Bank), in 168 BCE, the Hasmonean priest Mattathias and his son, Judah Maccabee, led a revolt against the Seleucidan despot Antiochus IV (who called himself Epiphanes, "the Risen God").

Antiochus sought to end Jewish religious and cultural separatism. He ordered the Jews to publicly renounce their beliefs, and commanded his troops to desecrate the Temple. A giant statue of Zeus was raised behind the Altar of Sacrifice; the Temple courts became the site of revels and destruction.

Finally the Jews revolted. It was during this rebellion that the idea of martyrdom took hold; to die *al-Kiddush ha-Shem* (to sanctify the Name, i.e., the Lord) became a virtue that would remain in Jewish consciousness for two centuries, until it was adopted by the Jewish Christians and eventually became a classic feature of Gentile Christianity.

The Maccabees' triumph in Emmaus in 165 BCE amazed everyone, including them. When Jerusalem was retaken and the Temple examined, the destruction was appalling and everyone despaired. The *menorah* was lit with what little oil could be found—and (according to the legend) lo, it remained miraculously lit for eight days until new oil could be obtained.

Hence the eight candles of the Chanukah *menorah*, the sculptural object par excellence of synagogue gift shops throughout the land. The tons of presents is an American elaboration. One irony is that, while Chanukah is considered a secular holiday (work is permitted), what drove the Maccabean revolt was a religious impulse.

15

THE OTHER HOLIDAYS

Rosh Hashanah. Yom Kippur. Passover. Chanukah.

Everybody knows what these holidays are about—or, at least, everybody (Jews, Gentiles, zombies, vampires) knows that they *are* Jewish holidays.

But what about Shemini Atzeret? What about Lag B'Omer? How can you tell others (and yourself) that you're a Real Jew if you don't know the difference between Tu B'Shvat and Tisha B'Av?

We're not saying you have to drop everything and celebrate each and every one of these holidays. (Although it couldn't hurt.) But you should at least know what you're not celebrating when you don't celebrate them.

There are other minor holidays observed in Israel but not so much in the United States, including Yom Yerushalayim (Jerusalem Day, 28 Iyar; commemorates the unification of the city of Jerusalem on June 7, 1967); Yom HaSho'ah (Holocaust Remembrance Day, 27 Nisan; commemorates the Jewish victims of the Nazi Holocaust and the Jewish resistance fighters); Yom Hazikaron (Israeli Memorial Day, 4 Iyar; honors Israeli armed forces and civilians killed by terrorists); and Yom Ha'atzmaut (Israeli National Independence Day, 5 Iyar; celebrates the Israeli Declaration of Independence on May 14, 1948).

Esther reveals to King Ahasuerus that she is Jewish and that evil Haman, his minister, proposes to kill her people. Haman is executed and the Jews are saved. Result: Purim, the only holiday in which noisy children are actually given noisemakers with which to make even more noise.

Many of the above celebrations have themes common to secular American holidays: harvest (Thanksgiving/Sukkot), disguises (Halloween/Purim), remembrance of wartime heroism (Veterans Day/Tisha B'Av), independence (Fourth of July/Passover), and trees (Arbor Day/Tu B'Shvat). So use those similarities if it helps you remember. Just bear in mind that what we don't have in the United States is a day of atonement. That's because we're Americans! We have nothing to atone for! At least officially.

Jewish Holidays

2010–2011 (5771)

Holiday	Jewish Date	Secular Date	Purpose
Rosh Hashanah	1 Tishrei	9 September	First day of the religious year.
Yom Kippur	10 Tishrei	18 September	Day of Atonement.
Sukkot	15–20 Tishrei	23 September	Feast of Tabernacles—harvest festival also commemorating the Jews' living in "booths" after the Exodus from Egypt.
Shemini Atzeret	22 Tishrei	30 September	Unclear. Traditionally celebrated as the eighth day of Sukkot, but is a separate holiday. Might have been cause for ritual prayers for rain.
Simchat Torah	23 Tishrei	1 October	Rejoicing Over the Torah—celebrates completion of a cycle of reading Torah in synagogue, after which the cycle begins anew.
Chanukah	25 Kislev	2 December	Dedication (aka Festival of Lights)—celebrates Jewish victory over Seleucidan despot Antiochus IV Epiphanes in 168 BCE.
Tu B'Shvat	15 Shvat	20 January	15th of Shvat—the New Year of the Trees. Trees planted throughout Israel.

(continued)

Holiday	Jewish Date	Secular Date	Purpose
Purim	14 Adar	20 March	Feast of Lots—celebrates events in the Book of Esther, in which Queen Esther helped save the Jewish people in the Persian empire from Haman, evil aide to King Ahasuerus—which no one is sure actually took place. (No evidence of Ahasuerus has ever been found.) It may have been instituted because Jews were surrounded by celebration of the Babylonian New Year, when their gods drew lots over humans' fates. *Pur* is Babylonian for "lot"; *purim* is a Hebrew plural. Who knows?
Passover (Pesach)	15–22 Nisan	19 April	Celebrates the Jews' Exodus from Egypt and redemption from slavery.
Lag B'Omer	18 Iyar	22 May	18th Day of Counting of the Omer—unclear what it celebrates. An *omer* is a measure of wheat used for sacrifice at the Temple. Some say it commemorates the end of a plague that killed 24,000 of Rabbi Akiba's students. Huh?

(continued)

Holiday	Jewish Date	Secular Date	Purpose
Shavuot	6–7 Sivan	8 June	"Weeks," thus, Festival of Weeks—celebrates Moses's receiving of the Torah seven weeks after the Exodus from Egypt.
Tisha B'Av	9 Av	9 August	Commemorates the destruction of the Temple in Jerusalem by Babylonians (586 BCE) and Romans (70 CE); the death of Bar Kochba after his revolt in 135 CE; the expulsion of Jews from England (1290 CE) and Spain (1492 CE); and other tragedies.

16

How to Not Accept the First Table You're Shown to at a Restaurant

In Hebrew school we're taught that the reason the Jews wandered in the desert for forty years after leaving Egypt was so that "the generation that grew up as slaves could die off, and the twelve tribes entering the Promised Land be populated by a people accustomed to being free."

The logic here is fuzzy, since everyone in those days lived forever. Moses himself, after four decades of shlepping and leading and bargaining with G-d and dealing with an entire nation's whining and complaining and overseeing numerous military actions *and* writing his Five Books, lived to the age of 120. This suggests that when he led the Exodus out of Egypt he was already eighty years young! They don't make them like that anymore.

In any case, the truth is, the Jews wandered because no one could agree with anyone else where to settle down. Some thought the Zered Valley was "nice" but others thought it was "ordinary." To some, Heshbon was "rustic" but to others, "the sticks." Og's kingdom in Bashan struck many as "touristy but fun," but a (vocal) minority called it "tacky." So they kept wandering.

This ethnic trait is evidenced today in restaurants all over the world, as Jews invariably decline to settle at the first able to which they are shown by a maître d', host, or hostess. You should do the same. But it's not enough, when refusing a table, to explain, "We're trying to be more Jewish" or "This is how our ancestors behaved after the Exodus." Rather, choose from these popular reasons for asking to be moved:

Primary Reasons for Not Accepting a Table

1. Too much noise. Jews hate noise. We say we "can't hear ourselves think," which actually means we're afraid *everyone else* can't hear *us* in our endless pontificating, lecturing, dispensing of words of wisdom and sage advice, and arguing about politics, food, and Israel.

2. There's a draft. Jews—a desert people, after all, and therefore more used to hot, scalding sandstorms—hate drafts of all kinds, whether icy blasts "from the air conditioner right on top of our heads" or a gentle, cool breeze "coming from some mysterious place somewhere." This is why Jewish mothers are always saying "take a sweater, just in case," which is a command disguised as a suggestion, and applies not only to eating in restaurants but also to going to concerts, baseball games (in August), Broadway shows, and the beach. All modern-day medical evils can be traced back to drafts.

3. It's too close to the kitchen. If sitting closest to the kitchen meant you'd get your food sooner, Jews would be fine with it. But it doesn't. Rather, it means being placed insultingly close to what seems sort of like a tradesman's entrance (even if the "tradesman" is your perfectly nice waitress), and being exposed to the harsh light and metallic clangor and shouted commands of the modern commercial kitchen. Plus all that coming and going through the double doors makes a draft.

These three reasons should be sufficient to get you moved at least two times to alternate tables. (See diagram on page 72.) In the event that more moving is necessary, or the host simply isn't buying your original explanations, try these:

Alternate Reasons for Not Accepting a Table

1. Those children are out of control. One's own children (and especially one's grandchildren) are, no matter how obstreperous or rowdy, "lively" and "precocious," and therefore a joy to behold. For some reason, though, when other kids behave the same way, it's intolerable. Bear in mind, however, that this excuse may not be properly delivered to a waiter or maître d' before first a) scowling at the offending children; b) rolling your eyes; and c) directing a patently phony smile of "understanding" to whatever adults are supposedly in charge of them.

2. The view is not so great. Jews like an unobstructed view of who comes in, what they're wearing, whom they're with, and what they order. This intelligence is essential for reporting back to the Bridge Club, the Mah-Jongg "girls," or the Canasta Group. It doesn't matter whether you belong to such a card-playing group or not. You might, one day, and this is good practice. And if you don't, you should.

3. You'd prefer another server. Jews tend to go to the same restaurants over and over. As a result we get very familiar with the staff and have opinions about all of them. Once a waiter or waitress makes a bad impression, there is simply no going back to his or her table. Use this one sparingly. You don't want to run the risk of alienating the staff of the restaurant unless it's absolutely necessary, or unless you know you'll never be coming back to this place anyway.

If you *have* alienated the staff, you might decide to reverse yourself on Reason No. 3 in the first list and sit as close to the kitchen as possible, to keep an eye on the preparation of your food. Forget it. Even if the kitchen doesn't have doors, or they're open, the people in there don't do the kinds of things you're worried about where customers can see. It's easier and safer to just be nice to the servers.

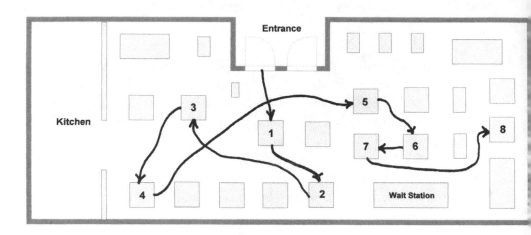

Reasons for Requesting Change of Table:

1. Too close to entrance.
2. Draft from overhead air conditioner.
3. Loud, ill-mannered children.
4. Too close to kitchen.
5. Obstructed view.
6. Too much noise.
7. "Cold air hitting me in the back of the neck from somewhere."
8. Perfect!

17
Circumcision: Take a Little Off the Tip

his is a controversial topic.

But not here! You literally cannot get more traditionally Jewish (if you're a male) than by having your foreskin removed. As G-d said to Abraham in Genesis 17, *10: This is my covenant, which ye shall keep, between me and you and thy seed after thee; Every man child among you shall be circumcised. 11: And ye shall circumcise the flesh of your foreskin; and it shall be a token of the covenant betwixt me and you.*

Easy for Him to say.

The arguments for and against circumcising babies seem both to have merit and to be overwrought. The practical (medical, sexual, hygienic) benefits of circumcision seem to be real but minimal. The psychological and sexual dangers seem to be possible but undocumented. Both sides, pro and con, have a ton of semi-conclusive proof to support their positions.

Eight-day-old baby on the morning of his bris, clearly oblivious to what is about to take place.

Were there Jews in Japan in the Middle Ages? Let's say
yes. And let's say that one was a Samurai.

Back in medieval Japan, the Emperor needed a new
Samurai to be his personal protector. So he issued a declaration, inviting the greatest swordsmen in all the land to
apply for this august position.

After interviewing a number of applicants, he narrowed
down the field to the final three: a Japanese Samurai, a
Chinese Samurai, and a Jewish Samurai.

The Emperor commanded the Japanese swordsman
to display his prowess. The Samurai took out a little box,
opened it, and out flew a bee. The Samurai made a single
deft movement with his sword, and the bee fell onto the
ground, neatly severed into two pieces.

"Impressive," the Emperor said.

Next it was the Chinese Samurai's turn. He, too, pro-
duced a small box. When he opened it, out flew a fly. With
two skillful strokes, the Chinese Samurai sliced the insect
into four equal parts, which fell to the ground.

"Even more impressive," murmured the Emperor.

Finally it was the Jewish Samurai's turn. He also brought
forth a box and, when he opened it, out flew a gnat. The
Jewish Samurai made a rapid series of strokes with his
sword and then stood back, as the gnat continued to fly
around.

The Emperor frowned. "You must have missed your target," he said. "The gnat is not dead."

The Jewish Samurai smiled. "Of course not," he said.
"Circumcision isn't fatal."

But if you're looking to shore up your sense of your own Judaism, you
should have it done, either in the hospital after delivery, or during a ceremony at home, eight days after birth.

That bris will prove to be the weirdest party you ever threw. Your parents (if they're alive, and Jewish) will *kvell*, your friends will find it both amusing and horrifying, and the baby will cry. If you're the baby's father, you'll feel ambivalent and proud and guilty. If you're the mother, you'll probably flee to an adjoining room if you don't pass out before you get there.

One thing you will be certain of, though: Those boys your son takes showers with, at summer camp and at the club and after phys. ed., will know that he's Jewish. Well, wait—lots of non-Jews get circumcised, too. Okay, they'll know that he *might* be Jewish.

Oh, and by the way: Circumcision has no sacramental significance. That means that an uncircumcised Jew is still a Jew. It's a tradition more than a requirement, although in Judaism it's hard to tell the difference between the two.

A Joke About Tradition

A young mother was making a brisket as her little daughter watched. "First," the mother said, "we cut off the end, and then we put it in the pan to get it all nice and brown."

"Why do you cut off the end, Mommy?" the little girl asked.

The mother thought for a second and then said, "It's just the way we've always made it. It's the way Grandma always makes it. It's what we call a *tradition*."

"But why?"

"You know what, Emily? I don't really know! Let's call Grandma and ask her."

So the young mother called *her* mother and asked, "Mom, how do you make a brisket?"

"Well," her mother said, "first you put it on the cutting board and you cut off the end, then you brown it in a pan with onions—"

(continued)

"I know that part," the daughter said. "But why do you cut off the end?"

"It's a tradition," the mother said. "It's just the way we've always done it." The daughter thanked her and hung up, but the older woman was vexed by the question. So she called *her* mother and asked, "Ma, how do you make a brisket?"

The old lady said, "Well, you put it in a pan—"

"Wait a minute, Ma. What about cutting off the end?"

"Oh," the old lady said, "I don't have to do that anymore."

"Why not?"

"I used to cut off the end because the best pan I had was too small. Then I finally got a bigger pan."

18

DIG THAT MESHUGGE KLEZMER!

orget rock, pop, country-western, show tunes, jazz, classical, chamber, world, and (insert here every other kind of music you know). If you really want to get down with the Chosen People you gotta avail your bad self of that funky *klezmer* sound.

What It Is

You've heard *klezmer*, if not live at weddings then on soundtracks or Web sites or "ethnic" compilations: The small, acoustic band of string instruments, woodwinds, and percussion, in modern times augmented with accordion, drums, even piano. The mournful minor keys. The long, sobbing intros suddenly snapping into zippy, peppy dance tempi. The beboppish speed of the solos. The lachrymose yearning of the violin cadenzas. It's zydeco for Hebrews, bluegrass for *landsmen*, Dixieland for Jews—

The name is derived from the Hebrew words *klei-zemer*, meaning, with boring literalness, "musical instruments." It started in Central and Eastern Europe in the late Middle Ages (see? They were good for *something*.) and early Renaissance, when itinerant Jewish musicians would travel from town to town in search of paying work—this, after a millennium of what

was essentially a ban on music (or, at least, on musical fun) following the destruction of the Second Temple in 70 CE.

Remember those days? You walked down the street whistling "The Girl from Ismailia" and everyone slapped you and went "shush." Thank G-d *that's* over.

For centuries, then, *klezmorim* (*klezmer* musicians) were limited to playing only at certain special occasions—weddings, Purim festivals, or the dedication of a synagogue. Go make a living, even in the Middle Ages, just doing that. And, as one source delicately puts it, "The *klezmorim* were, by temperament, restless and emotionally unstable individuals." Musicians? Restless and emotionally unstable? You don't say.

Restless and flighty or not, many of them were good—sometimes great—players. But they played by ear, since a proper musical education was usually impossible. Some of them were lone wolves, individual virtuosi who traveled from place to place with a minimum of entanglements with other musicians or, uh, regular people.

The most popular instrument among them was—if you can believe it—the hammer dulcimer, a flat, stringed instrument played with two padded hammers. (It's also called the *cembalo*, which suggests that the famous Jewish violinist Efrem Zimbalist Sr. descended from a *cembalo* player before himself begetting Efrem Zimbalist Jr., the star of *both 77 Sunset Strip* and—take that, J. Edgar Hoover—*The F.B.I.*! Although most Jews don't use "junior" and only name their sons after deceased relatives. Then again, Senior was a musician. You know how rebellious and restless and emotionally unstable they are.)

The tunes were dances, folk songs Jewish and non, reveries, and other found melodies. Over the past thirty years or so there's been a revival of

interest in *klezmer*, with great groups form-
ing all over the United States and the world.
Klezmer has never been more popular or
easier to find.

There's the Klezmatics and the Klezmorim and the Flying Bulgar Klezmer Band.
There's Beyond the Pale and Golem and
Brave Old World and Kroke and the provoc-
atively named Monsieur Camembert. And
others.

So by all means, get some *klezmer*, play
it through your earbuds or headphones
or boom box or Victrola or whatever you
use to listen to music, and revel in/burst
into tears over this distinctive Jewish musical
heritage.

You may like it. No, you may *love* it. You
may, in fact, become inspired to share it with
others. And if you do, here's an idea that's
just crazy enough to work.

Our Idea That's Just Crazy Enough to Work

Having been newly *klezmerized* yourself, you might think about bringing it to places in the non-Jewish (or not-entirely-Jewish) world where
people may never have heard it before. It'll be a *mitzvah*, although in
some cases it may also be a misdemeanor punishable by fine.

These suggestions require you bring a source of *klezmer* with you.
The authentic, albeit complicated and expensive, way to do this, of
course, would be to hire a band and truck them along to the various
destinations we mention below. This option will certainly be more fun
than the alternative—to put MP3s of *klezmer* on a player. You decide.
But if you go the iPod route, be sure to bring a cable that will let you
plug its output into external players.

Make sure your group can perform a broad selection of songs, dances, rhapsodies, and reveries, or put them on an MP3 player. Then do any or all of the following:

1. Go to a baseball game or football game held in a decent-size stadium; it could be minor league, college league, or even major league. Find the sound booth and either insist the engineer give your band a chance to wail, or pipe the recorded *klezmer* to the crowd at maximum volume for as long as you dare.

2. Go to a bar with a popular Karaoke Night. If you've brought your band, instruct them to join you at a table and have a few drinks, until people get used to their presence and stop gawking. At your signal, have them leap onto the stage and start playing. Or, find the sound system that plays the karaoke music and plug in your iPod. Then sit back and dare a roomful of drunken office workers to sing along. (Don't worry. They will.)

3. Do the same thing at a roller-skating or ice-skating rink: Find the source of the music, substitute your *klezmer*, and turn it up to TWELVE. Then stand back and watch skaters of all ages incur contusions, broken limbs, and pulled muscles as they chaotically strain to skate "to the music."

How will all this help you feel more Jewish? By enacting, with your itinerant wanderings and brief, lightning raids with *klezmer*, the roaming freelance gypsy musician lifestyle of the original *klezmorim*, that's how. You'll know how they felt (restless, emotionally unstable), and you'll make even less money at it than they did.

19

HOW AND WHY TO DEFLECT
A COMPLIMENT

ou're a sensible, enlightened, educated person. You're emotionally intelligent. You know that, when someone gives you a compliment, the odds are that they are *not* trying to manipulate you, deceive you, or tempt evil forces into harming you.

(You also know that this statement does not apply if you work in show business, which for these purposes includes movies, television, fashion modeling, popular music, classical music, dance, opera, the legitimate stage, fine art, cuisine, and local, state, and federal government.)

True, they may not really mean the compliment. It's possible they're just being polite. But that's nice, too. And so you do what any healthy, sane individual would do. You say "thank you" and perhaps you return the compliment in some equally sincere, or at least courteous, way.

That's why getting in touch with your inner Traditional Jew will often be harder than it looks. If you've done therapy or analysis, or taken part in any other kind of therapeutic investigation into your own personality, you know too much to be a Real Jew. You know that the reflex to be negative, to find the cloud behind every silver lining, is not a sensible way to protect yourself in a hostile world. Rather, it's a self-defeating, neurotic habit that can, and should, be brought to light, examined, understood, and eliminated.

This is an enlightened, intelligent, evolved series of insights, and you're going to have to unlearn them all if you want to get really good at deflecting compliments like a Traditional Jew.

Why? Because Real Jews, before the age of self-awareness, didn't trust compliments, for the same reasons they didn't trust good fortune. To them, good luck was the way Fate tricked you into letting your guard down, the better to leave you vulnerable to the inevitable bad luck that stalked everyone, whether they knew it or not.

Those people didn't say "thank you" when someone said something nice about them. Instead, like the superstitious peasants from whom they descended, they warded it off. They rejected praise. They shrugged and minimized and waved it away. They said *"Kain ein horeh!"* (or, colloquially, *"kenna-horra"*) to fend off the Evil Eye. In short, they treated a compliment like an insult, and an insult like a trivial matter of opinion. They knew that the best way to keep bad things from happening was to not get too complacent if something good happened, and better than that was not acknowledging that something good had happened at all.

And you can, too!

You can, and you must if you want to know what it feels like to be a Jew back when it really meant something. For the same reason you have to learn to be passive-aggressive (you probably don't want to see chapter 13, "How to Be Passive-Aggressive," right? No, that's okay. It's not really very good. . . .), you have to learn to dodge, repel, and deflect compliments.

Study the Basic Technique, below. Note these fundamental principles:

1. Each response consists of a physical gesture and a verbal reply. Practice applying both at once, so that each automatically elicits the other.

2. Each response is intended to make the person giving the compliment feel wrong. If at all possible, do not say "thank you." Even if you do thank the other person, however, you must immediately devalue your thanks by suggesting he or she is foolish, naïve, sentimental, etc.

3. Look for the gloomy side. No matter how nice the thing said, there is always a way to find something to complain about or feel oppressed by.

4. Each response does more than merely block the compliment. It demands sympathy. When you are able, automatically and without thinking, to convert the energy contained in a compliment into an equally energetic insistence on sympathy, you will know you have mastered the technique. (This—the immediate conversion of a nice thing said about a person into a reason to feel sorry for the person about whom the nice thing is said—is a classic example of the ancient Middle Eastern skill known as Jew Jitsu.)

Man on Left: Wow, Doug, you look great in that fez!

Man Wearing Fez: No, I don't. The only reason it fits is because my head is really shaped like this.

Deflecting a Compliment

Basic Technique

1. **When someone praises your clothes.**
   - EXAMPLE: "That's a lovely dress."
   Physical Response: Dismissive shrug.
   Verbal Response: Allude to some invisible problem.
   "It's too small/big/etc."
   "I'm freezing."
   "It costs a fortune to dry-clean."
   "This *shmatteh*?"

2. **When someone praises your hair.**
   - EXAMPLE: "Did you get your hair done? It looks great."
   Physical Response: Roll eyes.
   Verbal Response: Suggest effect is temporary.
   "Wait until I wash it. It'll never look like this again."
   "Right—until I sleep on it."
   "It has a mind of its own."

3. **When someone praises your cooking.**
   - EXAMPLE: "These meatballs are delicious."
   Physical Response: Dismissive wave.
   Verbal Response: Devalue the praise.
   "Did you read that article about ground beef? We should all be vegetarians."
   "I ran out of oregano. Don't tell me you can't tell."
   "The recipe was for ground lamb. Good luck finding it in the store."

4. **When someone praises your home.**
   - EXAMPLE: "Is this new furniture? It's beautiful!"
   Physical Response: Grasp forehead, shake head in agony.
   Verbal Response: Announce your oppression.
   "Three weeks old and already it's impossible to keep clean."
   "Please. Finding the right accessories is killing me."
   "I'm afraid to get it dirty. I do everything in the bedroom now."

5. When someone praises your child.
- EXAMPLE: "Your daughter is a lovely young lady."
  Physical Response: Deadpan look of rebuke.
  Verbal Response: Claim victimhood.
  "Lovely is as lovely does."
  "You obviously weren't around when we discussed her grades with her last night."
  "To anyone but her parents, yes."

TIP: Use the Physical Response as a stalling device to buy yourself a second or two in which to think of the Verbal Response.

If you need more time, employ either the Eye Roll of Long-Suffering Martyrdom or the All-Purpose Fatalistic Shrug and Pursed Lips Suggesting Inevitable Defeat to keep the other person hanging on your every word until you come up with something suitably negative, pessimistic, and/or accusatory.

20

So You Want to Have an Opinion About . . . Islam

There's a familiar good news/bad news split vis-à-vis having an opinion about Islam. The good news is, all of us, Jewish and not, know more about Islam than we used to. The bad news is in the way we found out about it and the reasons we may have had for learning more about it.

All the more stark and, one might say, poignant, then, does this render our desire to explore our ancient traditions by adopting an opinion about Islam from an earlier and, one might say, more innocent era, as,

for example, 1956. (Wasn't that a stirring, but hard-to-read, sentence? See chapter 11, "How to Write and Speak Like a Rabbi.")

To do this—to bring our opinions about Islam more in line with what our forebears thought back when no one had even yet seen *Lawrence of Arabia*—let's first establish what contemporary Jews think about Islam today.

In general, as basically educated, media-reading-and-listening-to-and-watching, nonspecialist, "ordinary" people, we *as Jews* think:

Contemporary Way to Think About Islam

✡ Islam is not, per se, our or Israel's enemy. Certain Muslims may be, but don't tell me it's an "inherently violent" religion. All religions have a history of violence. "Read the Koran!" Oh, yeah? Read the Book of Joshua. For that matter, if you want "violent," read what G-d does in the Torah, or what, per the Book of Revelation, Jesus supposedly will do at the end of the Tribulation. If Islam were inherently and unavoidably violent, you'd have 1.3 billion adherents attacking everyone else in the world. Although you probably wouldn't, because it would probably have brought about its own destruction centuries ago.

✡ Which doesn't mean they don't have their warring sects driven by their own parochial *meshugass*. The Sunni, the Shia—those people may feel justified (or inspired, honored, etc.) in killing each other, but to us they're both equally nuts, or at least "nuts" in the way that everyone considers everyone's religion except their own. Of course, if you believe you'll go to Heaven by becoming a martyr, then killing and risking being killed over dogma becomes a reasonable thing to do. But we don't believe that. In fact we think that that, too, is totally nuts. It's also morbid.

✡ The 9/11 terrorists, the suicide bombers, Al Qaeda, the Taliban: How much are these terrible people driven by Islam, versus something else? How much is it political, with people using religion—unconsciously, let's say—as an excuse to grab for power or to act out resentment? How much is it historical? How much do they "hate the West" because they feel humiliated economically or materially? For that matter, how much is their feeling "humiliated economically or materially" a rationalizing gloss on deeper, more personal emotional problems? In general, how much do violent individuals use Islam (or any religion) as a pretext and an excuse?

✡ Islam is inherently no better or worse than any other religion. Many of its beliefs are, to us, absurd, but so are the founding myths of Christianity and so are the miracle stories of the Old Testament. Most of its practices are weird (rioting over the publication of a cartoon comes to mind), but not all of them. And, as always, what we think about them, they think about us.

✡ We can deplore how they treat women, we can express bafflement at their rejection of alcohol, we can cheer or stay silent in the face of their taboo about eating pork—in the end, it's their business. If their women want to protest and reform things, *ess gezunterhait.* Meanwhile, if Muslims keep to themselves, what do we care? We know the world is full of *meshugass* and we have some of our own. In any case, Islam Shmislam. We have plenty of other things to worry about.

You can see the hairsplitting and hoop jumping one goes through to be fair. To return to your ancient roots, forget all your carefully balanced, nuanced positions. Try this on for size:

Traditional Way to Think About Islam

✡ Who? Islam? Is that the same as whatchamacallit in India? Hindu? What's Buddhism, then? Is that the fat man who sits under the tree?

✡ Islam—is that the one with the gods with all the arms? And the elephants? What am I thinking of?

✡ What's "Moslem"? Is that it? "Muslim"? Is there a difference?

✡ Oh, you mean like with the Arabian Nights. Scheherazade? That mystical Oriental type of thing?

✡ They're the ones who pray facing Mecca! The man goes up to the top of that tower and blows a bugle and everyone stops and falls to their knees. They what? They keep kosher? I thought only we did that. Are they Jewish?

✡ What is the difference between Islam and Arab? *Is* there a difference? Aren't all Arabs Muslim? Except no, you hear on the news about Arab Christians and Druze, whatever that means. So Islam is a religion. Okay. They don't have a pope, right? Believe me, it's just as well. One is enough.

✡ Mohammad? Is he like Jesus Christ? He's the Jesus Christ of Islam?

✡ Oh, he's a prophet! Like Elijah. Okay. And G-d is Allah, right. And all this happened when? AFTER CHRISTIANITY? You're kidding. Not before? In 632? CE? Who invents a religion after Christianity? Besides the *farkakteh* Mormons, I mean. Look, you want my opinion? *Never mind.* It's for those people. Over there. They're in . . . wherever they are. Arabia, India, Egypt, Iran, whatever. Why should I even think about them? If I were in Israel, okay. But this is America. Here we have Jews, and we have *goyim*. Isn't that enough?

21

LET'S *GET* A TRADITIONAL DIVORCE

Sure, to inspire your lackluster, all-American denatured Jewishness, you could get married (*already*), and in the Orthodox manner: men and women separated, public reading of (and existence of) the wedding contract known as the *ketubah*, bride and close relatives making a candlelit circuit seven times around the groom, newlywed couple hoisted aloft on chairs, etc. But that's the obvious thing to do.

Instead, let's approach the subject from the other direction, as though reading from right to left. If you're looking to call it quits, you should think about having a nice, old-fashioned Jewish divorce. It isn't easy, but a) if it were, everybody would be doing it; and b) divorce never is anyway.

This process revolves around something called a *get*. No, not "get" meaning "the obtaining of a prestigious guest for a talk show," as in, "Queen Elizabeth was on *Letterman* last night. What a get! Rather, *get* is an Aramaic word for a document of divorce.

What is outlined below may seem punishingly elaborate, but if it weren't, you wouldn't cherish it as much. And women! Be glad we're not telling you to go about it in strict accordance with Biblical writ, because back then—and you can't get much farther "back" than "then" and still remain in the Bronze Age—the man had all the power. He could, per Deuteronomy 24:1 (*When a man hath taken a wife, and married her, and it come to pass that she find no favour in his eyes, because he hath found some uncleanness in her: then let him write her a bill of divorcement, and give it in her hand, and send her out of his house.*), just hand his wife the I-divorce-thee *get*, and she got git.

Happily—or, at least, less miserably—as far back as the Second Commonwealth (530 BCE–70 CE), actual practice in matters of divorce was more humane and less unfair, paternalistic, and, frankly, obnoxious than actually specified by the written law. Men couldn't *really* just divorce their wives on a whim. And if they asserted they could, they were reminded that, to do so, they had to both refund the bride's dowry and pay her the marriage settlement as specified in the *ketubah.*

There were, however, two absolute grounds for the dissolution of a marriage: unfaithfulness (see chapter 9, "Use the Bible to Tell if Your Wife Is Unfaithful") and childlessness. If, after ten years, no child had been born, the husband was not only permitted to divorce the wife, but he was required to.

Custom was accorded a kind of secular legal legitimacy when, in 1000 CE, Rabbi Gershom ben Judah convened a synod in Mainz, Germany, where it was decreed that divorce must entail mutual consent. It was also decreed that a Jew could not read another's private mail, and could not be polygamous—proving that, even a thousand years ago, life was a good news/bad-news proposition.

The *Get*

The *get* must be handwritten by a *sofer*, a qualified scribe, specifically for the couple involved. Thus, a *get* is the only document in the universe for which there are no downloadable forms. It can be in any language, as long as it contains the key words and phrases required by Jewish law. Of course, you'll prefer yours to be in Aramaic. Traditionally it consists of twelve lines, with the witnesses signing below the twelfth.

In addition—and in *halakha*, or Jewish law, there is always something "in addition"—the *get*:

✡ Must be written on a fresh document, without the possibility of erasing or changing the text.

✡ May not be written on anything attached to the ground—for instance, a fig leaf. (see chapter 45, "Learn the Kabbala (or Make Your Own!)," for a medieval incantation to summon the Devil that not only could be written on a leaf, but had to be!)

✡ May not be predated.

A minimum of seven people must be present for the ceremony of the divorce to be valid: the husband, the wife, two "kosher witnesses," and

"Ruth, please. Stop working for two minutes and face reality. This is the *get*. Don't touch it until I put it down. And hurry up. The rabbis and those two teenagers are waiting."

a *beth din,* a court consisting of at least three rabbis. Since "kosher," in this case, refers to "male, Torah-observant adults," you're looking at a setup in which one woman is divorced, judged, and witnessed by six men. That can't be easy.

Oh, and since "men" means "males over the age of thirteen," you are possibly talking about a situation in which a woman's divorce is not considered legitimate or final unless it's witnessed by two eighth-grade *pishers* younger than her children. If there is such a thing as an Ortho-dox sitcom, *there's* a plot in which hilarity could possibly ensue.

The witnesses, in fact, are more than mere passive observers. In a sort of medieval anticipation of Heisenbergian advanced physics, the divorce does not actually take place unless the witnesses are there to observe it. So ladies, be nice to all Jewish boys over the age of twelve. You may need their validation one day.

One fun part of the *get* proceedings involves what may appear to be a sort of party-game-like practice in which the man, after first filling in his portion of the document, sort of throws it to, or flips it to, or drops it into the hands of, the woman, so that she may fill out her part.

The idea behind this, other than to inadvertently provide some levity to what is otherwise at best a melancholy occasion, is to prevent the two parties from touching the *get* at the same time.

In some cases, if either the husband or the wife is unable to personally attend the ceremony, they may appoint an agent to represent them. This appointment process itself, you will not be shocked to learn, requires a proceeding before a *beth din.*

As the wording of the *get* stipulates, once the ceremony is complete, the (now ex-) wife is told she is "permitted to all men." G-d forbid it should say, "All men are permitted to you." But it's only 2010 CE. These things take time.

22

WORRYING I

How to Worry

ot only have today's assimilated Jews forgotten how to worry, but they've actually decided that it's best to not worry at all. And just like that: the techniques and skills refined by generations of neurotics and hysterics, *gone*—thrown out the window by a fancy-schmancy generation too busy with therapy, yoga, twelve-step programs, and antidepressants to stop and think for one second just what they're doing to the legacy of the great Jewish worriers of old.

And then they wonder why they don't really feel "all that Jewish."

Look, we're in favor of mental health. But at what cost to tradition, custom, folk identity, and U.S. sales of Tums? Our forefathers didn't *shlep* out of Egypt and drag themselves across the desert for forty years so that, thirty-five hundred years later, their descendents could sit back on their duffs and raise a glass of Diet Pepsi and say, "Here's to not sweating the small stuff."

On the contrary: If you're sweating it, it's not small stuff. It's Jewish-reality stuff. And you should be sweating all of it, all the time. Worrying is how we know we're alive—and Jewish. Sure, some people deal with a stressful situation by doing what they can about it and then letting it go. And if you want to walk around feeling like an Episcopalian, that's what you should do.

If, however, you want to connect with your ancient (i.e., twentieth-century) Jewish past, you'll bear in mind the fundamental fact that Real Jews never let go. So study the chart below. Memorize its lesson about how to convert a Non-Jewish, Healthy Response to a given issue into a Traditional, Worry-Based Response.

Better yet, make a copy of it or cut it out and keep it with you at all times. If you have trouble remembering these lessons, or even though you have the table right in front of you and are reading from it, you still have problems doing what it recommends, see several doctors immediately. Something terrible may be wrong with your eyesight or your brain.

Conversion Table
Non-Jewish Response to Worry-Based Response
(Clip and Save)

Non-Jewish, Healthy Response to Issue	Traditional, Worry-Based Response to Issue
Let it go.	Hold on to it with both hands.
Take it easy.	Think of the worst thing that could possibly happen and react as though it already has.
Don't fly off the handle.	"Don't tell me to 'chill out,' this is serious!"
Live in the present.	Obsess about the past and fear the future.
Neutralize anxiety and reassure others by focusing on what is real and what is actually happening.	Maximize discomfort and drive everyone around you crazy by getting hysterical, predicting disaster, and insisting that someone call the police, then throw up your hands because you have no idea what to do.

Of course, the above chart offers only a theoretical approach to proper Jewish worrying. For a more hands-on approach, you need to learn the two major schools of Jewish worrying. They are explained below.

Type 1—Worrying About Yourself to Yourself

The most effective strategy for worrying about yourself to yourself, in a traditional Jewish manner, can be boiled down into three short words: *Expect the worst.*

Expecting the worst is not only *a* way to worry, it's the *only* way to worry. If you're not expecting the worst, you're not really worried. You're "concerned." Concern is for the *goyim*; worry is for the Jews.

Which means don't mess around. Take things to their theoretical limit and then keep going. The following chart offers some examples.

From Bad to Worse

Inflating Reasonable Concern into

Authentic Jewish Worry

Inciting Incident	"Concerned" Response	Authentically Jewish Worried Response
You sneeze.	"I guess there's pollen in the air."	"Christ, it's swine flu. Now what?"
Your doctor says, "I'm going to send you in for a blood test."	You think, "Really? How interesting. I wonder why—maybe some cholesterol thing."	You think, "Oh G-d. How much time do I have left?"
Your boss, while passing by your desk, says, "Hey, after lunch, stop by and see me for two minutes."	You think, "Huh. I wonder what's up?"	You think, "That's it. I'm fired. I'll never get another job, we'll lose the house, and we'll have to move in with my parents."

How do you know you're doing it right? You'll *feel* it. It's not that you'll be visited by a vague intuition, that something inside you will suddenly say, "Yes, this is it. At last I'm worrying in the correct Jewish manner."

You'll literally feel it. You'll get hives. Your stomach will turn into a volcano. You'll experience what commercials in the early sixties—back when men were men and worriers were worriers—used to call "distress in the lower tract." You'll have the sensation of something pressing against your inner eyeball.

You will have put so much stress on your body that you will have made yourself physically ill. At that point, pour yourself an Alka-Seltzer and wish yourself a hearty *mazel tov*. You have attained the plane of Master Worrier and are worthy to be called a Jew-di Knight.

But: Should you talk about it? Should you share your anxiety with others? No-but-really-yes. Even (and especially) if no one asks about your suffering, *hint* that something is wrong. Hint like crazy. Sigh deeply for no apparent reason. Stare moodily into the distance at inappropriate times in the company of others. Begin to say something, then suddenly stop, and when someone says, "What? You were about to say something," reply, with maximum bravery and fake sincerity, "No. It's nothing."

This ploy has a twofold benefit. One, it enables you to worry without releasing your worry into the atmosphere, where it will thus lose all its life-robbing, traditional Jewish corrosiveness. Two, it offers a convenient opportunity to practice being passive-aggressive.

(For more on being passive-aggressive, see chapter 13, "How to Be Passive-Aggressive." Or, all right, fine. *Don't* see it. Do whatever you want.)

Type 2—Worrying About Others at Others

No, that's not a mistake. You should worry not only about others, but *at* them.

Worry Type 2, like Type 1, can be reduced to basic principles. However, because this sort of worrying involves at least one other person, the requisite number of steps is greater:

1. Expect the worst to happen to the other person.
2. Tell them that in as hysterical a manner as possible, preferably before they ask you.

3. Be twice as upset when they refuse to agree with you.
4. Reject their efforts to get you to calm down.
5. Hint—broadly—that, in the end, the person who will suffer most from this will be you.

Note how the above sequence of steps consists not of worry on behalf of someone, but of using worry about someone *on your own behalf.* That's why it is described it as "worrying at" someone. You don't sympathize with them. You inflict your worry *on* them, treating them like a basketball backboard or the wall of a racquetball court. Your worry about them bounces off them, so to speak, and comes back to involve (and worry) you.

Man worrying. His expression suggests that he may be worrying about the fact that he's worrying, which is a cause of concern.

The following Sample Dialogues illustrate this process. In each, imagine that you are the worrier.

Sample Dialogue A: Two Girlfriends Talking on Phone

Worrier: How are you?
Person B: Fine. You know. Tired.
W: Have you seen a doctor?
B: [laughs] No, I'm going to take a nap—

W: Really? It could be chronic fatigue syndrome. That's all I need, is you confined to a bed for the next ten years.

Sample Dialogue B: Two Men Playing Golf

Worrier: Hey, did you ever call that mechanic you asked me about?
Person B: Nah, it's the Check Engine light. I'm just going to ignore it.
W: Jesus, is your marriage that bad? That you're, like, flirting with suicide?
B: Who said anyth—
W: You don't want to use that mechanic, fine. But I'm not going to sign off on your killing yourself because you have fights with your wife. I don't want that on my conscience.

Sample Dialogue C: Mother Talking to Teenage Son

Worrier: What's this?
Person B: It's a B in calculus.
W: I thought you studied.
B: I *did* study.
W: Is this what it's going to be? We spend a fortune sending you to this school so you can get into Yale, and you're just going to piss it away?
B: What—how do y—Most people got C's!
W: Most people always get C's! That's what a C *is*! Fine. You know what? You go to Dumbbell State with most people and major in parties. I'll just tell my friends that you're "trying to find yourself." Then, when you're on welfare and can't get a job, you won't need calculus anyway, so it'll all work out and I'll stop banging my head against the wall.

The more you worry about others for their own good, the more you get to worry about yourself. It doesn't get any more traditionally Jewish than that.

23

WORRYING II
What to Worry About

In order to become a more Jewish Jew, it is not enough that you only alter your worrying technique. You must also change the nature of the things you worry *about*.

The topics on the minds of everyone today—the economy, the health-care system, and so forth—are, to be sure, all worthy of the general public's concern. And that's the problem. They're not Jewish enough. If you're writing blog comments about hybrid cars or letters to the editor about talk radio, you're living in a reality-based real world of the present. And that's what we're trying to correct.

The quickest way to explain the difference between your current worries and the new (i.e., old) ones we suggest you adopt is via the following chart.

Conversion Chart of Contemporary Worries to Traditional Worries

Forget Worrying About This	Instead, Worry About This	Don't Say This	Instead, Say This
Global warming	Getting to Miami for the winter	"The ice pack in Antarctica is melting."	"I need new sweaters for all the air-conditioning down there."

Forget Worrying About This	Instead, Worry About This	Don't Say This	Instead, Say This
Economic crisis and recession	Being charged for High Holy Day tickets	"Everything is frozen because the banks aren't lending."	"Fifty dollars for two seats? What is this, the Rocky Marciano–Jersey Joe Walcott fight or Rosh Hashanah?"
Life savings lost to Bernie Madoff	Dropping a bundle on Las Vegas Night at the synagogue	"The whole nest egg was in his fund. Gone."	"I know it goes to the Sisterhood, but who keeps losing and still plays roulette for three hours?"
U.S. health-care reform	Quotas at medical schools	"No, the public option *is* the 'compromise.' The insurance companies are *ganefs*."	"Of course they deny it. But read the names of who gets admitted. You think there are only three smart Cohens in the whole country?"
Islamic terrorism	Anti-Semitism in the Soviet Union	"Bin Laden isn't Ghengis Khan. He's Al Capone. Those people are criminals, not an army."	"Don't let the bald buffoon *shtik* fool you. Khrushchev didn't get where he is by being amusing."

(continued)

Forget Worrying About This	Instead, Worry About This	Don't Say This	Instead, Say This
Super-virus	Tay-Sachs disease	"Look, it's a race—mutation versus drug research to find a cure."	"Look, we're a race. Let's hope there's drug research to find a cure."

Pharaoh practices Moses's Jewish worrying style. "Sure! Lead your people to the Promised Land. Meanwhile, who's going to finish all those pyramids?"

24
How to Give a Backhanded Compliment

entile adage: "If you can't say something nice, don't say anything at all."

Jewish adage: "Not saying anything at all is out of the question. So say something not-nice by pretending to say something nice."

The proper delivery of a backhanded compliment is an essential skill for renewing your connection with your classic Jewish roots for two reasons.

The first resides in the fact that Jews have a cultural mistrust of unalloyed praise. Saying that anything is good tempts the Evil Eye—the metaphysical force of tragedy that lies in wait to oppress the Jews at all times. Thus, praising someone invites catastrophe on the praiser, the praisee, and anyone in the immediate vicinity.

Second, middle-class American society today is so relentlessly positive, so saturated in "support" and "self-esteem" and "affirmation," it has become extremely difficult for Jews to perform their traditional societal role as neurotic overachievers. How can a person drive himself crazy with self-loathing and insecurity in spite of his manifest accomplishments if everyone around him is offering sincere congratulations and empathetic understanding?

Praising people with backhanded compliments addresses this problem.

How to Do It

To someone not versed in the giving of backhanded compliments, it looks difficult. But don't worry. You're perfectly capable of learning how, no matter what people say about you.

Step One

Compose the compliment. This will be easy. You'll see someone do a praiseworthy thing, from bringing home a good report card to getting a promotion to making a great meal, and you'll instinctively feel an impulse to say nice things about it.

Step Two

Pinpoint the problem. It can be either personal (i.e., your problem with the person) or general (that is, a hidden pitfall with the accomplishment). And don't worry that you won't be able to think of one. There's always a problem. If the person just did X, why can't she do Y? If he's been recognized for something, you "only hope" he can keep it up. If someone's outfit looks good, it's because it conceals or modifies something not-so-good. There is no silver lining without its cloud. "You won the lottery! Great—now you have to find an accountant you can trust. Good luck." Etc.

Step Three

Deliver the backhanded compliment. Combine the result of Step One with that of Step Two in a way that not only seems to make sense, but in fact seems to embody a higher order of wisdom.

As you'll quickly learn, nothing is so wonderful or praiseworthy that it can't be used against someone. Study these examples:

	A Earned Compliment	+ B The Problem	= C Backhanded Compliment
Wife to Husband	"Congratulations on your raise."	He gets to work with adults, while you're stuck at home with children all day.	"At least the people *you* work with act like they appreciate you."
Husband to Wife	"This pot roast is delicious."	All she has to do is cook and boss the kids. You're the one under pressure all day.	"I *knew* you had it in you to make something good."
Mother to Child	"Good job! You got a hundred on your algebra test!"	She's impudent and mouthy and can't be bothered to show the slightest bit of responsibility.	"You're so good at math! Maybe now you can figure out how to clean your room once a month."
Father to Child	"You were brilliant in your piano recital."	She (and her brother) are a couple of self-involved ingrates who don't know how good they have it.	"That concert was great. Who was the girl right after you? She was really something!"
Child to Parent	"That trip to Florida we all took was really fun."	They boss you around and don't give a damn about your feelings.	"I can't wait to go to Miami all by myself!"

(continued)

	A Earned Compliment	+ B The Problem	= C Backhanded Compliment
Friend to Friend	"You look good after having lost thirty pounds."	With her rich husband, she does nothing but shop and work out all day.	"It couldn't have been easy to lose that much weight! And, believe me, with your life, it'll be hard just to keep it off."

"Wait a minute—what did he mean just now by 'You're not half as dumb as you look'?"

25

CHILLIN' AND ILLIN' WITH *TEFILLIN*

In our quest to break through the constraints of our secularized, assimilated American fabulousness and reassert our ancient Hebraic nature, sometimes eating chicken chow mein or *kvelling* over Eddie Fisher records just isn't enough. Real Jews occasionally feel the need for something truly exotic, mystical, and strange. And in *tefillin* they have found it.

Or them. *Tefillin*—the word can be singular or plural—are small leather boxes, about two or three inches on a side, affixed to leather straps. Inside are strips of parchment on which are inscribed four passages in Hebrew, from Exodus 13:1–10 and 11:16, and Deuteronomy 6:4–7 and 11:13–21. You—assuming you are an Orthodox Jewish male over age thirteen—fasten one to your inner arm and one on your forehead prior to chanting the morning prayers every day except Sabbath and on holidays. You needn't do this at a synagogue; you can *bentch* (pray; recite a blessing) *tefillin* at home, at school, and even at work.

Which is, let it be said, arguably a bit weird. This is, after all, not a garment, not an elegant or complementary enhancement of the human form, like breastplates or special hats or robes. These are a pair of objects, props that you wear, stubby blocks that stick out of you while you festoon yourself with a bunch of leather straps. It's one thing to enshrine a prayer or two in a little box on the entrance to your home (see chapter 5,

"How to Obtain and Mount a *Mezuzah*"), which amounts to a small object adorning a much bigger object. It's another thing to strap it to your *head*.

But the ungainliness may have been part of the original point. The English word used to refer to *tefillin* is "phylactery," which derives from the Greek *phylakterion*, which means "fortress" or "protection."

"Fortress" and "protection" suggest that at least part of the original function of *tefillin* was to serve as an amulet, a charm against enemies and hostile demons. So no wonder they looked, and continue to look, weird. If you're sporting a device harboring magical powers in order to ward off invisible (or visible, human) enemies, you want it to look unusual.

Why We're Willin'

The obligation to wear *tefillin* comes from Exodus 13:9: *And it shall be a sign unto thee upon thy hand, and for a memorial between thine eyes, that the law of the land may be in thy mouth.* It is possible that all of Judaism throughout history might have taken this commandment too literally, in which case, oy. What if "a sign upon thy hand" just meant "like, a ring or something"? And what if "a memorial between thine eyes" meant "remember this in the memory of your brain inside your head"?

Then again, Deuteronomy 6:8 reaffirms, with regard to *these words which I command thee this day,* that *thou shalt bind them for a sign upon thine hand, and they shall be as frontlets between thine eyes,* so forget that other theory.

Anyway, leather boxes. One is affixed to the inner arm just above the elbow (the side of the arm closest to the heart) after a ritualistic winding of the straps around the forearm, the palm, and the fingers. The other, which is the more sacred of the two, is worn at the apex of the forehead.

Each box contains four passages from the Torah:

1. *Kadesh* (Exodus 13:1–10)
2. *VeHayah Ki Yeviacha* (Exodus 13:11–16)

3. *Shema* (Deuteronomy 6:4–7)
4. *VeHayah Im Shamoa* (Deuteronomy 11:13–21)

In the arm *tefillin*, these are on a single scroll; the box is a uniform cube and mounted on straps with a big slipknot. The strap of the head-piece is a fixed loop and the box is divided into four sections, each of which contains an individual scroll with a single Biblical passage.

You may as well know that the leather thus employed can only be from an animal that has been considered ritually "clean." The sewing on each is limited to twelve stitches. And if you're thinking, "I guess the thread used for sewing them up is . . . what—some kind of cotton-poly blend?" the answer is, "No, the thread must be made of the dried veins of a 'clean' animal."

These days—i.e., ever since the fourth century—*tefillin* are worn only by Orthodox Jewish men in the morning. Prior to that, many Jews wore them as part of their daily apparel, until open hostility toward Jews prompted our forebears to appear on the street sans phylacteries.

Tefillin are unnecessary on the Sabbath and festivals, the rabbis believed, because the holidays themselves provided enough signs and symbols of religious identity to render wearing them redundant. It goes without saying that there are highly codified rituals to be followed in creating them, putting them on, and taking them off; the sixteenth-century systematized code of rabbinic law, the Shulchan Aruch, includes no fewer than 160 laws covering how they're made and used.

Not like this.

Women, as usual, need not apply.

How to Don and Doff *Tefillin*

Putting on *tefillin* is just about as methodical and prescribed as you'd think, but it could be worse. For video instruction, and to hear the blessings involved, go to YouTube and do a search for *tefillin*. But here's a brief description, which alone should convince you that, if you're looking to reestablish (or establish for the first time) a connection to the ancient ways, you've come to the right place:

Be sure you're standing. Then start with the arm—use your stronger arm to tie it onto the other arm. Put your arm through the loop on which the box is mounted, then place the *tefillin* itself on your biceps just above the elbow—of the left arm if you're right-handed, and vice versa if you're a southpaw. Close your forearm as though doing a dumbbell curl, until it holds the box in place. Then say the blessing, which goes:

בָּרוּךְ אַתָּה יְיָ אֱלֹהֵינוּ מֶלֶךְ הָעוֹלָם

אֲשֶׁר קִדְּשָׁנוּ בְּמִצְוֹתָיו וְצִוָּנוּ

לְהָנִיחַ תְּפִלִּין

Which is to say:

BARUKH ATAH ADONAI, ELOHEINU, MELEKH HA'OLAM
    ASHER KIDISHANU B'MITZ'VOTAV V'TZIVANU L'HANI'ACH T'FILIN

Move the box slightly so that it rests on the inside part of the arm, then tighten the slipknot until the *tefillin* remains in place. Then wind the straps twice around your upper arm (which will yield three wraps in total), and then, as though winding a barber pole, spiral the strap around your forearm from the elbow toward the wrist, seven times.

Warning: This is a ritualistic act, not a surgical procedure or a sadomasochistic exercise. You don't get extra spiritual points for tightening the straps to the point where they hamper your circulation. Jews have suffered enough.

Like this.

You've still got a lot of strap left. Wind it around your left palm a couple of times, then pick up the headpiece.

This, though more sacred, is much easier. Position the *tefillin* at the point of your forehead and be sure its framing straps are split, one on each side. Adjust the head strap around the upper circumference of your head so that the box stays in place. If you've spoken since you said the first blessing, you have to say another, slightly different blessing:

בָּרוּךְ אַתָּה יְיָ אֱלֹהֵינוּ מֶלֶךְ הָעוֹלָם

אֲשֶׁר קִדְּשָׁנוּ בְּמִצְוֹתָיו וְצִוָּנוּ

עַל מִצְוַת תְּפִלִּין

BARUKH ATAH ADONAI, ELOHEINU, MELEKH HA'OLAM
ASHER KIDISHANU B'MITZ'VOTAV V'TZIVANU AL MITZVAT T'FILIN

and

בָּרוּךְ שֵׁם כְּבוֹד מַלְכוּתוֹ לְעוֹלָם וָעֶד

BARUKH SHEIM K'VOD MAL'KHUTO L'OLAM VA'ED

Back to the hand: Unwrap the excess strap from the left hand, then loop the strap around the base of the middle finger once, then around the upper part of the same

Wrap firmly but do not impede circulation. Note how upper-arm winding forms the letter *shin*.

finger, and then once more around the bottom part. Wrap the remainder around the palm and say:

וְאֵרַשְׂתִּיךְ לִי לְעוֹלָם

וְאֵרַשְׂתִּיךְ לִי בְּצֶדֶק וּבְמִשְׁפָּט וּבְחֶסֶד וּבְרַחֲמִים

וְאֵרַשְׂתִּיךְ לִי בֶּאֱמוּנָה וְיָדַעַתְּ אֶת יְיָ

V'EIRAS'TIKH LI L'OLAM
V'EIRAS'TIKH LI B'TZEDEK
UV'MISHPAT UV'CHESED UV'RACHAMIM
V'EIRAS'TIKH LI BE'EMUNAH
V'YADA'AT ET ADONAI

—and you're ready to say the morning prayers.

In all instances, be sure the shiny black sides of the straps are facing out, and loosen any kinks that may have developed. If you've done it properly, you will have created the Hebrew letter *shin* along your upper arm and created—more or less—the Hebrew letters *daled* and *yod* on your hand.

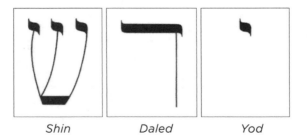

Shin　　　　Daled　　　　Yod

Put together, these are the letters of the name of G-d. The whole procedure is somewhat finicky. But it's not arbitrary.

Take the straps off in the reverse order and put them away.

You should handle them carefully not only because they're sacred objects, but because, according to a Lubavitcher rabbi, a pair of kosher *tefillin* run around $350. Ever buy an Empire chicken? No one said kosher was cheap.

26

THE ORIGINAL BAM!

The Basics of Mah-Jongg

How inevitable that there be, in a book dedicated to reawakening the over-assimilated, highly diluted American sense of Jewishness, a chapter on a Chinese parlor game whose variations include versions from Hong Kong, Sichuan, Taiwan, Japan, Singapore, and Vietnam, and something created by the Royal Australian Navy called Pussers Bones.

Yes, let's talk about Mah-Jongg. This is the American spelling. It can also be spelled "mahjong." However you spell it, you may be thinking, "Chinese food for Jews, okay. But *Mah-Jongg*?"

It's a good question. Another good question is, "What's so reasonable about Jews craving Chinese food?" Especially considering that many Chinese dishes focus on those two ultra-*trayf* (nonkosher) ingredients, shrimp and pork, and there has never been *a single Chinese recipe for brisket.*

Chinese food was covered in an earlier chapter. Now, let's address the issue of exactly how the heck Mah-Jongg got so identified, in the United States, with Jewish women.

As Tevye says in *Fiddler,* "I'll tell you. I don't know."

No one does. It's not even clear how and when Mah-Jongg originated in China. Some think it began as a variation of a card game played during the early Ming Dynasty, in the late fourteenth century; others, that it was invented by army officers during the Taiping Rebellion (1850–1864), or by a nobleman living in the area around Shanghai in the 1870s, or that brothers from Ningpo adapted the ancient Ming card game around 1850.

In any case, in 1920 Abercrombie & Fitch brought Mah-Jongg to America. It became a wildly popular fad, acknowledged and spurred by Eddie Cantor's hit song "Since Ma Is Playing Mah-Jongg." Even then, in the earliest years of its Americanization, Mah-Jongg was mainly played by and associated with Jewish women. Why?

There is no definitive answer, but one theory points to the fact that New York's Lower East Side was then (and still is) contiguous with Chinatown. Perhaps the Jewish wives and mothers of the time, newly arrived immigrants for whom a leisurely, highly social table game offered a pleasant opportunity to strengthen community ties (not to mention a chance to gossip and *kibbitz* and *nosh* and *shmooze*), were easily exposed to and fascinated by the exotic Chinese motifs and materials of Mah-Jongg. So sensible and appealing is this theory that it is almost certainly wrong.

However Mah-Jongg got started, one can see its tactile appeal. The tiles are *neat*: thick wood, plastic, ivory, or even bone rectangles, more colorful than dice, more satisfying in the hand than dominos, with pretty and enigmatic letters and symbols. The clatter of the tiles is much more pleasing than the ho-hum slap of cards. Indeed, one theory of the game's history holds that its name derives from the Chinese word for "sparrow" or from "clattering sparrow." In any case, anyone who has ever fetishized a set for backgammon, chess, go, or even checkers can understand Mah-Jongg's equipment appeal.

As for learning how to play Mah-Jongg, the good news—to the extent that Mah-Jongg involves anything that can be called "good news"—is that, as far as we can see, Mah-Jongg is a lot like gin rummy. Who knew? It works thus:

The tiles come in three suits—the bamboos, the circles (or stones), and the wans (characters). There are also "honors" (four winds and three dragons), four seasons, and four flowers.

The idea is, as in gin, to collect and discard tiles, one at a time, in order to amass groups or runs of three or four tiles. You can create a *chow* (a consecutive sequence of three tiles of the same suit), a *pung* (three identical tiles of the same suit), or a *kong* (four identical tiles of the same suit). You always have the same number of tiles (thirteen in this version) until you are ready to—get this—"go Mah-Jongg."

Going Mah-Jongg doesn't mean entering some state of dementia or abandon, as in "going insane" or "going commando." It means you call out, in a gin-like fashion, "Mah-Jongg!" to declare you've won the game. At that point you will have accepted a fourteenth tile to complete your hand.

The special tiles, the special hands, the rules, the arcane terminology, the clockwise rotation of the assignment of winds, with east wind being dealer—all this would call for an entire book itself, such as *The Red Dragon & the West Wind,* by Tom Sloper, which makes a great gift for someone who has just become a *bubbe.*

Unlike, say, chess, Mah-Jongg is subject to a huge number of regional interpretations and variations of play. The National Mah-Jongg League, formed by Jews in 1937 and still going strong, publishes an annual card updating the official American rules and sanctioning a new series of winning hands.

There are international Mah-Jongg tournaments and a World Series of Mah-Jongg, held in Macao. There is also a North American tournament held by the NMJL's younger rival, the American Mah-Jongg Association, which fittingly climaxes at that pseudo-international pseudo-Mecca so beloved of East Coast Jews, the Trump Taj Mahal hotel casino in Atlantic City. Playing Mah-Jongg at the Taj—*that's* Jewish.

All of which means that, should you decide to reinvigorate your Jewishness by learning Mah-Jongg, you'll be in thriving and plentiful company. And it wouldn't be Jewish without a warning of potential disaster. Doctors in Hong Kong recently released a study concluding that extensive playing of Mah-Jongg can induce epileptic seizures.

27

REASONS, IN SPITE OF EVERYTHING, TO STILL HAVE A BAR MITZVAH

First: All of what follows applies to girls, too. Just change the "r" in Bar to a "t."

You want to get more in touch with your traditional Jewishness—and, more important, you want your son to get in touch with his. So you want him to have, or be, or become, or whatever the verb is, a Bar Mitzvah.

But there's a problem. Half of the meaning of this ceremony has become, as the *alter kakers* used to say, *kaput*. Now what?

First, a brief review. The term *bar mitzvah* means "son of the Commandment," and refers both to the ceremony and to the boy, age thirteen, at its center. This noble, joyous, and yet nonetheless serious ritual—

Okay, everybody knows it celebrates the moment when the seventh- or eighth-grader "becomes a man." After this glorious event, the little *pisher* is supposedly, per tradition, allowed to help comprise a *minyan* (the quorum of ten Jewish men necessary for praying in public), he has to wear *tifillin* for chanting morning prayers, and he is allowed to be one of the three men required in order to recite grace after meals.

Or so it was, and maybe still is, in Orthodox circles. (If the newly minted adult wants to seek out an Orthodox congregation in which to strap on phylacteries [see chapter 25, "Chillin' and Illin' with *Tefillin*"] and *daven* [pray] with the other men, they'll be happy to receive him. Maybe. If they honor Conservative or Reform Bar Mitzvahs. They might not. In fact, they probably don't. So just forget the whole thing.)

In America, today, where Conservative and Reform Jews outnumber the rest, Bar Mitzvah boys (and their parents) all enjoy a good laugh

Biblical-era boy gives Bar Mitzvah speech to congregation. ". . . And I especially want to thank my Uncle Mephibosheth and my Aunt Zelophehad, who camelled all the way here from Hormah."

at the notion that a middle-school kid barely old enough to shave is a "man." And if the rabbi has a sense of humor, so will he. Or she.

No matter how splendidly the Bar Mitzvah boy recites his Maftir (the part of the weekly Torah portion he sings before the congregation) and/or his Haftarah (a selection from the prophets), he will not be able to drink, drive, or have sex without incurring disgrace, disapproval, and possibly punishment until he is of legal age. Likewise, no matter how mature, thoughtful, and well delivered his speech, he will not be able to vote, join the armed services, legally get into an R movie alone, or do much of anything else other than show up at school the following Monday for that Algebra 1 quiz he and all the other "men" and girls have to take.

If the community isn't going to treat him like an actual adult man, and if he's not going to feel like an actual adult man, then what's the point? Why should you want him to have a Bar Mitzvah and how can you convince him to do so?

Here's why: Because, even if the social meaning of the event is archaic and obsolete, giving your son a Bar Mitzvah reaffirms your membership in the community of people who gave their sons Bar Mitzvahs.

So, man schman. Do it to renew you're a Jew. And below are not only three more benefits you derive from helping your son be a Bar Mitzvah *bucher* (student), but several reasons to present to him in order to get him to go along. *Mazel tov!*

Reasons for a Bar Mitzvah: For the Parents

1. You get to shut up your parents or in-laws who wonder if your son "really knows he's Jewish." It's not the only reason, but it's a nice side benefit.

2. You get to demonstrate to your son that you're proud of him by displaying that to the world. He won't appreciate it, but when does he ever? Still, you can try. Unless he explicitly asks you not to have a Bar Mitzvah for him, he'll notice it if you don't—especially if he has Jewish friends who, week after week, are inviting him to theirs.

3. You get to flaunt it. The image of the overdone Bar Mitzvah, with the lavish reception, the pricey eats, the stars of Cirque du Soleil at the reception, the appearance of Li'l Kim for the kids and the London Philharmonic for the adults, is a tired cliché. Which doesn't mean you can't do it. If you want to show family, friends, and business colleagues that you've had worldly success, or you want to look as though you have, this is as valid a pretext as any.

Reasons for a Bar Mitzvah: For the Kid

1. You can do it even if you're an atheist. It's a social ritual more than anything else (see No. 2, below). Of course, you may decide, in the white-hot passion of your proudly held atheism, that it would be hypocritical of you to take part in so primitive a ceremony. But a) your parents might still insist; b) it will deepen your education; and c) you'd obtain all the other benefits on this list.

2. It's an acknowledgment of puberty. Okay, you're not a "man." But you can look that congregation in the eye and say, "Today I am a teenager." And that's the next best thing. American society doesn't have a formal initiation ritual for entering puberty, which is why so many American men, Jews and Gentiles alike, grow up into big overgrown boys. But during the few hours of your Bar Mitzvah, your parents and other adults have to at least pretend you're more than a child.

3. You get to feel, in a small way, like a big shot. Everybody has a birthday, so ordinary birthday parties confer at best a bogus kind of celebrity or glory. "Yay me! I was born!" But for this occasion you'll have learned at least some Hebrew, and you'll have chanted it in public, and you may even have written and delivered a speech—all of which (probably) will be unique to you and unduplicated by your peers. You will feel, for once, that you've earned the applause, no matter how much you cheated, memorized the Hebrew phonetically off an MP3, phone in the speech, and don't really mean any of it.

4. You get stuff. Not only from the usual sources—parents, relatives, and friends—but from your parents' friends, who otherwise wouldn't be caught dead at one of your birthday parties. That means money, gifts, etc., of an order of magnitude larger than a normal birthday haul.

5. You won't have to do anything else for your parents for another five years. Then you'll have to "get into a good school," which will require real work. So live it up while you can.

Going to Bat for the Girls

It should go without saying that the list above, "For the Kid," holds true for a Bat Mitzvah, too. Although that ceremony is less common than its male counterpart, and the absence of one means much less for the girl than for the boy. Look, if your daughter has her heart set on being a Bat Mitzvah, go for it. You and she will realize all the benefits mentioned above, *and* you'll feel (and be seen as, and actually *be*) egalitarian, feminist, and enlightened.

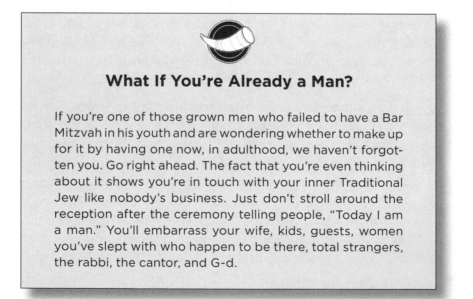

What If You're Already a Man?

If you're one of those grown men who failed to have a Bar Mitzvah in his youth and are wondering whether to make up for it by having one now, in adulthood, we haven't forgotten you. Go right ahead. The fact that you're even thinking about it shows you're in touch with your inner Traditional Jew like nobody's business. Just don't stroll around the reception after the ceremony telling people, "Today I am a man." You'll embarrass your wife, kids, guests, women you've slept with who happen to be there, total strangers, the rabbi, the cantor, and G-d.

28

INTRODUCTION TO *HONDLING*

Here's exciting news: If you've ever shopped at a flea market or bought something off Craigslist, you may already have *hondled* and not even known it.

Hondling is Yiddish for "negotiating"—but not "negotiating" as in striving to reconcile rival factions to achieve a workable peace in the Middle East, or coming to terms on a new union contract. No, *hondling* means dickering for a decent price on something you're buying, whether an item (like a bracelet) or a service (like painting a living room).

Hondling isn't as prevalent today as it was in earlier, preindustrial societies, but it does live on in contemporary settings such as farmers' markets, garage sales, and car dealerships and, of course, buying a house. Still, there are many Jews (and other ethnic groups from the Middle East) who can't buy anything from anyone without striving to get the best bargain they can *hondle*.

Most clerks in retail stores will, alas, be unable or not permitted to *hondle* back. In fact they'll find one's efforts at *hondling* to be anywhere from insulting to insane.

Tough! Who asked them? We urge readers who want to reinvigorate their Jewishness to return to the practice of *hondling*. Over anything—a pair of shoes, a slice of pizza, an appendectomy. Whatever. This approach to consumerism should have particular appeal to our

Men *hondling*. The fact that both seem to have forgotten what they are *hondling* about does not stop them.

conservative readers, since there is no purer expression of the market than when seller and buyer slug it out in real time until they reach a mutually acceptable price.

Note, however, that not all *hondling* styles are the same, and vary according to the personality of the *hondler*. Some are straightforward, others more oblique. See which one works best for you.

The Guerrilla *Hondler*: Aggressive, no-nonsense, preemptive, obnoxious. Strikes quickly before the salesperson knows what hit him or her. Sample dialogue:

Checkout Clerk: Hi! How are you today?
Guerrilla *Hondler*: [points to item] How much is this?
Checkout Clerk: The English muffins? [examines item] Oh! Here it is. Three forty-nine.
Guerrilla *Hondler*: Yes, but how much for *me*?

Bear in mind that the Checkout Clerk in such a situation is likely to say (after, "Huh?" and "Are you serious?") things like, "For you? Um, same as it is for everyone. Three forty-nine." Don't worry about it. Just respond with a quick counter. "I'll give you three dollars." If the clerk refuses, nod in acceptance and continue with the purchase.

Even if the clerk refuses your every offer to *hondle*, do not be apologetic or embarrassed. This is *business*.

The Passive-Aggressive *Hondler*: Shrewd, intuitive, plays on the emotions of the other party. Rather than being confrontational about bargaining, this *hondler* seeks to manipulate the other party by denigrating *him-* or *herself*. Sample dialogue:

Jewelry Store Salesperson: May I help you?

Passive-Aggressive *Hondler*: Oh, I don't know. This . . . it's just so beautiful. In fact it's just what I've been looking for all my life, but . . .

Jewelry Store Salesperson: But what?

Passive-Aggressive *Hondler*: I . . . I just can't buy it for myself. It's too luxurious. I don't deserve it.

Jewelry Store Salesperson: Of course you do!

Passive-Aggressive *Hondler*: But this price . . . it's set deliberately high to chase away people like me—people who really aren't worthy of this kind of extravagance. . . .

Ideally, at this point you want the salesperson to say, with great warmth and reassurance, "Well, not so fast. Let's see what we can do." Sadly, this rarely happens. Instead, note the salesperson's probable response and the Passive-Aggressive *Hondler*'s counter:

Jewelry Store Salesperson: I'm sorry. But this *is* the price.

Passive-Aggressive *Hondler*: Oh, that's all right. It's not your fault. I'm sure there's nothing you can do . . . even if you wanted to. . . .

Jewelry Store Salesperson: It really isn't up to me.

Passive-Aggressive *Hondler*: Oh, I know. If it were, you would have taken a little off the price and sold it. And I would have bought it! [bitter laugh] Not that I could ever get up the nerve to *wear* it, of course . . .

Jewelry Store Salesperson: It's not really a question of "nerve."

Passive-Aggressive *Hondler*: Not to you, maybe. You're a healthy, confident person. I mean, it was hard enough for me to decide to pay more than I can afford, but just the idea of wearing this piece makes me all . . . I dunno . . . scared.

Continue in this vein. Compliment and flatter the salesperson by criticizing and despising yourself. The idea is not only to elicit sympathy, but to imbue the salesperson with a grandiose sense of power and magnanimity, from which exalted standpoint he or she will condescend to take a little off the price. It might work.

The Reverse-Psychology *Hondler*: Canny, tricky, this *hondler* relies not on eliciting sympathy or pity but on cultivating fellow feeling and mutual respect between *hondler* and salesperson. Sample dialogue:

Department Store Salesperson: Are you interested in the watch?

Reverse-Psychology *Hondler*: Are you kidding? This is so great. And you're *right* to charge this much. I could never afford it—but don't lower the price one penny! It's absolutely worth it. If not more! I wish I could pay that kind of money. What a great life I'd have if I could.

Department Store Salesperson: It is a handsome piece. . . .

Reverse-Psychology *Hondler*: You know who it would look good on? You.

Department Store Salesperson: Oh! Well . . .

Reverse-Psychology *Hondler*: I mean it. It suits your style.

Department Store Salesperson: It would look good on you, too.

Reverse-Psychology *Hondler*: You really think so?

Department Store Salesperson: Absolutely. Here, why don't you try it on?

Reverse-Psychology *Hondler*: Oh, I don't know. . . .

Department Store Salesperson: Let's just see.

Reverse-Psychology *Hondler*: Well—okay. . . . [tries on watch] You're right. It's fantastic. Okay, I'll take it. But on one condition. You gotta knock a little off the price so I don't feel like I've gone completely insane.

Will this work? Who knows? But it's worth trying. By applying reverse psychology, you become "friends" with the salesperson, then try to sell the watch to him or her, and then, when they resume trying to sell the watch to you, hold out as though you're doing them a favor in buying it. With that one small proviso.

29

LEARN TO WHISPER SO THAT EVERYONE CAN HEAR YOU (AND THEN DENY THAT YOU "SAID ANYTHING")

In the sixties and early seventies one of the most pejorative things you could say about a person was, when they expressed an opinion, that they were "making a value judgment." Example:

Person: Oh wow, did you see the Airplane on Dick Cavett? Balin was stoned out of his gourd and Grace was, like, way not into it. It's like nobody could get it together.
You: That's a value judgment!

Back then, making a value judgment was considered (by those under the age of, say, thirty-five) a social and philosophical faux pas. You weren't supposed to *judge* people. It sounds naïve today, but back then—at least according to the counterculture subscribed to by America's youth at the time—you were supposed to live and let live.

Where did this peculiar ethos come from? One of its sources was middle-class Jewish high-school and college kids. These young people rejected not only the cultural and, in many cases, political opinions of their parents, but their elders' habits of being aggressively opinionated, too. It was an obvious target for rebellion, because having opinions is what Jews *do*.

To the post–World War II generation of American Jews—i.e., the parents of the sixties generation—having opinions but suppressing them led to ulcers, neuroses, alcoholism, and the need for tranquilizers to fend off "a nervous breakdown." The idea of not having any opinions at all, or feeling that you shouldn't have any, was tantamount to converting to Buddhism.

This attitude was best demonstrated by the mothers of the young people of the time, suburban Jewish housewives with active minds and tart judgments and no one to share them with during the day except the kids, i.e., a couple of little *pishers* who couldn't care less. You place someone like that—someone both opinionated and, probably, insecure, which is what leads to being opinionated—into the deluxe solitary confinement of suburban life and something sooner or later is going to explode.

In their case, the explosion took the form of "whispered" comments in public places (restaurants, synagogues, theater lobbies, country club dining rooms, etc.), the subjects of which were not only "accidentally" able to hear them, but were *intended* to hear them. If the whisperer was then chided by a companion (a husband, a friend, a child), she responded with a display of operatic disingenuousness unshakeable in its (pseudo-) innocence.

And that's what you have to learn to do, if you want to really recapture your traditional Jewishness. You have to be able to snipe cattily about someone in public in such a way that it seems you don't want them to hear you, but that assures that they *do* hear you—and then, when someone objects and tells you to "be nice," to deny that you "said anything."

It won't be easy. These days everyone, of whatever generation, is merrily unconstrained when it comes to making value judgments—although we no longer call it that. We call it "speaking out," "expressing yourself," and, somewhat more pejoratively, "being judge-y." But certain principles of etiquette continue to apply. It's still rude to be loudly outspoken, to snipe and snip at someone in public with your negative opinions. These tenets, as everyone knows, are the basic, fundamental rules of civilized comportment.

Tough. If you're really serious in your quest to reconnect with the

Girl in Foreground with Hot Dog: "Look, Sam, I know she's your sister. I just don't know why she has to wear her hair like a giant head of kale. . . ."

ancient ways, you must learn to break these rules—or, at least, bend them until they beg for mercy. Here's how.

Basic Technique

The Whisper: First, the term "whisper" is not to be taken literally. An actual whisper would be inaudible to its subject, and thus defeat the purpose of the exercise.

When you see someone whose attire, behavior, looks, marriage, home, children, hospitality skills, etc., you disapprove of, lean partially toward your Supposed Confidant (i.e., anyone in your party whom you will pretend to be talking to) and say, *in a perfectly normal voice*, your Judge-y Remark.

A "perfectly normal voice"? Not a stage whisper? Yes. Bear in mind that your public vocal tone is—or should be, if you're a suburban Jewish mother—louder and more urgent and vivacious than your private manner of speaking. Therefore, using a normal voice in a public setting *seems*, relative to what one normally expects, discreet. It plays as whispering, while remaining audible over a range of at least ten feet.

Your remarks can be delivered in any one of a wide variety of attitudes, including but not limited to:

- Snide: "She's got to be kidding with those tits."
- Disingenuous: "Is it true she kicked him out of the house?"
- Sarcastic: "Whoever told her green was a good color for her was certainly a genius. . . ."
- Openly disapproving: "Have you seen the addition they put on? *Hideous.*"
- Semi-complimentary: "Well it's better than her usual hair. . . ." (See chapter 24, "How to Give a Backhanded Compliment," for delivering this remark directly to its subject.)

There is virtually no limit to what you can criticize, mock, deplore, or judge. What matters is that *you appear to be trying to be discreet.*

The Attitude of Wounded Innocence: After you've announced your opinion, your companion(s) will in some way signal you to be quiet. There are two appropriate responses to their trying to get you to shut up. Both begin with the Unjustly Accused "What—?"

1. Pretend that you don't know what they're protesting. Say "What—?" as though to say, "What are you chiding me for? What have I done wrong?" Open your hands and spread them apart in the universal gesture of bewilderment.

2. Pretend that you think they simply disagree with your judgment. Say "What—?" as though to say, "What, don't tell me you see it otherwise . . ." Then say, indignantly, "It's true!" as though they're taking issue with your accuracy and not your rudeness. Nod sharply to convey the certainty that, while your companion doesn't have the courage to face the truth, you do.

To these your companion will say either, "You *know* what. Now shush," or "Never mind 'it's true.' Shush." At that point you should bristle, move around in your seat (if you are sitting), or ostentatiously look away (if standing) as though physically trying to regain your composure after absorbing their insult, and generally act as though you're the one being wronged.

It's not as easy as it looks. At first your tendency will be to feel too embarrassed to say anything at all, or to murmur a criticism that no one else can hear, or to blurt out your opinion but shrink away with "never mind" when challenged.

Fight these tendencies and keep practicing. This is how our Jewish forefathers (or, at least, foremothers) interacted with the members of their community. Keep at it and see if, in time, you don't feel like a housewife in Pikesville (Baltimore), Larchmont (New York), Cheltenham (Philadelphia), Port Washington (Long Island), Shaker Heights (Cleveland), Silver Spring (Washington, D.C.), or Encino (Los Angeles) in 1962.

30

HOW TO BUILD A SUKKAH

ukkot, as everyone knows, means "booths," and *Chag ha'Sukkot* means "Festival of Booths." If you think this refers to a celebration of trade conventions, you're even less Jewish than we feared. All the more reason, then, for you to bone up on your *sukkah* skills and then get out there and build one yourself.

The holiday of Sukkot (which can be rendered as Sukkos and Succoth, and is also known as the Feast of Tabernacles) began as a harvest festival similar to those celebrated by many of the cultures and civilizations surrounding the Jews. With the arrival of the Torah, Sukkot became one of Judaism's three pilgrim festivals, during which the men and boys of all the tribes would journey to the Temple in Jerusalem, per the instructions of G-d as delivered in Exodus 34:23 (*Thrice in the year shall all your men children appear before the Lord GOD, the God of Israel*). Kind of like the Super Bowl, with the Biblical equivalent of big foam fingers and tailgating.

During the seven days of Sukkot, at synagogues and at Jewish homes around the world, people gather to eat (and, in some cases, to sleep) in handmade little shelters (or booth, hut, etc.). The edifice can be constructed in the backyard, on a porch, or even on an apartment's balcony. Its purpose is to commemorate the crude homes in which the children of Israel lived during their forty-year sojourn in the desert after escaping Egypt, when nobody had a backyard, let alone a balcony with a view.

There is, of course, a wealth of custom and lore regarding the *sukkah*, such as the fact that when rain falls, one is not required to stay inside it. "Oh, good," you think, but not so fast. It's not that custom takes pity on the Jews about to get drenched. Rather, the interpretation (in the Mishnah, a compilation of the Oral Law passed down after the Torah was complete, which forms one of the Talmud's three sections) is that, for whatever reason, G-d is so displeased with us that He won't allow us to fulfill our obligation of remaining in the *sukkah*.

All the more reason to stop stalling and go build one.

The Old-Fashioned Way

How hard can it be? You're not making a fixed dwelling, but merely a shell that you should be able to disassemble quickly and haul through the desert for four decades. It should be big enough to accommodate a table and chairs, and sleeping bags, if you want to go all the way.

The *sukkah*'s walls can be constructed of virtually any material, including aluminum. To be built to code (i.e., in accordance with *halakha*, the combination of Biblical and Talmudic law and tradition), it must have at least two and a half walls, whatever that means, and it must be at least three feet tall. You can even use prefab lattices, those crisscross panels used to make wall trellises and gazebos. Here's how.

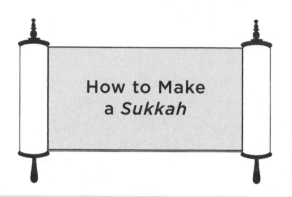

How to Make a *Sukkah*

You'll need:

A second person
Sixteen 2′ x 8′ lattices
Eight 1″ x 2″ x 8′ pieces of lumber
Four cinder blocks
Four 6′ pieces of rope
One hundred 75-lb. cable ties—those plastic zip-things with a little buckle at one end. You stick the pointy end through the buckle, pull tight, and it stays. It's what cops (at least on TV and in movies) use to bind the hands of "perps." Their ties are too lightweight for this, though. You'll need somewhere between standard and light heavy-duty grade ties.

1. Lay two lattices next to each other with the long sides touching. Loosely lash them together with four cable ties along their length.

With one of you holding the two lattices at a right angle, tighten the ties so they remain at that angle. But leave a little play in them so you can fold them up when the holiday is over.

2. Do this with the seven other pairs of lattices. You now have eight hinged, right-angled pieces.

3. Place one hinged piece flat on its side. Place another four feet away, facing it. You now have two L-shaped pieces facing each other, like benches without legs. Take a third piece and set it as though it is sitting on both benches, at one end, with its right-angled piece touching the backs of the benches. Tie these along their intersecting lines to form a square arch. Leave it on the ground.

4. Do the same with two other right-angled pieces and a third piece to connect them. You now have two square arches.

5. Stand the two arches up eight feet apart. (You'll need another person and maybe a stepladder.) Take a third hinged lattice unit and connect the two arches: Lay one side of it on top of the two uprights, with the other side hanging down. Lash securely all along their connecting points. If you've ever used or seen an erector set, this will seem a gigantic version of that, but in wood.

6. Do the same with another L-shaped segment across from the one you just did.

7. You now have a giant parson's table—four uprights, four hinges connecting them around the top—without a roof. This is the basic *sukkah*.

8. Frame each doorway with the lumber by lashing the wood to the edge of each entrance. This is for structural rigidity.

9. Place a cinder block on the ground in each corner and lash it to the walls, for ballast in case it's windy.

10. Decorate with branches, fruit, gourds, tree limbs, etc. Be sure to leave the roof open enough to see the stars at night.

11. If you want to be very strictly *halakic* (legal), consult a local authority on whether it's kosher to have four doors. If it isn't—and this seems to be a judgment call—get more lattices and tie them across the bottom half of the non-door openings (from the ground up), to create windows.

12. Trim the cable ties so they don't look all spiny and weird. You may need some stout cutters if the ties are too thick for regular shears.

13. After the holiday is over, disassemble in reverse order. Cut off and discard the ties lashing the L-shaped pieces to each other but *do not cut the ties that have formed the L-shaped pieces themselves.* You want to end up with eight L-shaped, hinged pieces you can fold in half and store.

This is not to say that our forefathers used lattices and cable ties, but don't kid yourself. They would have if they could have, and it's entirely permitted. One additional benefit of using lattice, apart from its low cost and light weight, is that its very gridlike design makes it easy to hang decorations on.

As for the roof, it must be of organic material (wood, bamboo, palm leaves, etc.) that once grew from the ground but is now disconnected from it. The roof should provide more shade than sun, but it must be porous enough to allow rain to enter—presumably so that G-d has a way of demonstrating His displeasure in case . . . well, just in case.

The New, Modern Way

There are, you will be semi-stunned to learn, many different prefab kits for building *sukkahs*, from the bare bones (braces, instructions, shopping list for the lumberyard—$55 and up) to the complete package of structural materials, walls, roof, the whole *schmeer* ($450 and up).

They come in a wide and amazing variety of styles. Some look like garden sheds hermetically wrapped for chemical decontamination; some, like army field hospitals covered with Jewish gift wrap; some, like gauzy cabanas. One (popupsukkah.com) even magically explodes into being like a combination high-tech camping tent and magician's prop. And it's kosher!

In any case, to each his or her own. But remember, if you go this more convenient route, make sure that the kit has proper rabbinical certification. The last thing you want to buy and build is a bogus *sukkah*.

Decorating the Sukkah

Central to the symbolism of Sukkot are "the four species" which, while it sounds like the name of a Darwinist doo-wop group, refers to the *lulav* (the closed frond of the date palm), the *etrog* (the citron), the *hadass* (myrtle), and the *aravah* (willow). The *sukkah* is decorated with these, and with other harvest-themed, seasonal things, like those weird, gnarled little gourds one has no idea how (or even whether) to eat, and whose purpose seems to be nothing more than to force people to harvest them in order to symbolize the harvest.

Once you've included these required accessories, you are free to customize your *sukkah* as you see fit. Here are some tips for achieving various looks in your booth:

Biblical: Go Old Testament with sand on the floor, oil lamps, and goats.

French Provincial: Herbs, herbs, herbs! Bundles of thyme, branches of rosemary, etc. Plus mirrors, embroidered pillows, and—because French Provincial homes in the seventeenth century didn't have closets—an armoire.

Modern: Just combine any of these words: bold, asymmetry, polished, surfaces, strong, geometry, clean, lines, neutral, colors. Thus, use bold surfaces with strong asymmetry in clean colors along neutral lines. Form follows function—just like it did when the Jews wandered in the desert for forty years.

Postmodern: The same as Modern, but add either a sundial or a floor lamp shaped like a Greek column.

Shabby-Chic: Anything from a bunch of yard sales.

31

So You Want to Have an Opinion About . . . ANTI-SEMITISM AND HOLOCAUST DENIAL

This topic may surprise you. Who *doesn't* already have an opinion about anti-Semitism (one of the elder patriarchs of despicable prejudices) and its psychotic baby brother, Holocaust denial?

To refresh your memory: The anti-Semite hates (or, in the genteel, sophisticated upper-class version, disdains) Jews based on a series of a priori assumptions about "how Jews are." The Holocaust denier takes all that a step further and flatly asserts that the systematic, industrialized murder of six million Jews in World War II Europe didn't happen.

Surely you don't need advice on how to have an opinion about such people. What's to discuss?

Well, not so fast. What if you could take your opinion and *turbocharge* it? What if you could, by strategically modifying that opinion, tap into the SOURCES OF ANCIENT POWER that, all your life, have remained HIDDEN in your CULTURAL PAST?

It sounds too good to be true, but the secret lies in the (pseudo-) scientific principle of DE-SOPHISTICATIONIZATION™.

You see, as an educated, psychologically astute person of the early twenty-first century, you hold opinions informed by an awareness of the cultural and historical forces that can influence someone's personality, values, and behavior. You know, for example, that what makes someone an anti-Semite or a Holocaust denier so loathsome is, *to a certain degree,* not their fault.

Say some idiot on a blog or in a fringe video interview says, "Well, it's obvious the Jews control the media, so of course they're in cahoots with the Jews on Wall Street." You know that this individual, like all bigots, is, to some extent, fundamentally ignorant. He's a victim of economic, cultural, and historical forces he knows nothing of. He's resentful, frustrated, and angry. Such feelings, of course, require release. He can't just sit there and suffer. He has to blame something or somebody.

At first he might be tempted to blame himself. His lousy job (or his lack of any job), his dreary marriage, his money woes, his disobedient kids, the general fact that the world today seems incomprehensible to him but is a subject of amused snickering to others—can it be all his fault? But there are ample voices in this great country of ours ready, on both a professional and an amateur basis, to assure him that it isn't. It's someone else's fault—the liberals, minorities, the "feminazis," the government, the Democrats, Hollywood, the "socialists" . . . and the Jews.

So he seizes on a theory that suits his intuitions and that is reinforced by those around him. The voice you hear when he speaks his mind is not just his. It's also that of his influences, his authorities, and his ignorance.

You know this. And your knowledge serves to qualify your opinion of him. "Yeah, he's a jerk," you think and/or say. "Then again, look at him. . . ."

This multifaceted awareness, this informed assessment, this subtle, nuanced opinion: It may be admirable, it may be compassionate, it may speak well for your intellectual honesty.

But wake up.

It's sapping your mind of valuable mental energy. It's hobbling your emotional life with pesky ambivalence. It's paralyzing you with self-contradictions.

It's holding you back!

You must regard these people (and that's what they are—"these people") not as you currently do, c. 2010 CE, with the mitigating understanding that comes from higher education, but as our forebears did in the previous century, before everyone went to a smarty-pants college and started learning about "society."

We call it De-Sophisticationization. And it's just what you need. Freeing up all those mental and emotional resources will not only make them available for more fruitful activities, such as impressing people at parties with your forcefully advanced views, but it will also enable you to issue thundering denunciations and stirring condemnations just like a Biblical patriarch. Won't that be fun?

A Contradiction

You may have already detected a contradiction in the above explanation.

"Wait a second," you may have thought. "All that psychological sophistication that makes me ambivalent and slightly understanding toward those anti-Semite *shmucks*; all that self-awareness and erudition and Talmudic balancing of the one hand versus the other—isn't that Jewish, too?"

You're right. It is. There is literally nothing more Jewish than education, learning, and intellect. So bear in mind that you needn't turn into a dumbbell just in order to be happier. Rather, merely shave off a little here and there to make your opinions of certain people (people who are, after all, *your mortal enemies*) a bit more streamlined.

Here's how.

De-Sophisticationization for Beginners

"De-sophisticationization" is a long, complicated word for something that at bottom is really quite simple. It is, in the world of judgmental moralizing, what pass/fail is in the world of pedagogy. Someone is either "okay" or "no good." There is no middle ground, gray area, or mixed feeling.

To the extent that it involves having access to your innermost emotions and expressing them with as little censoring as possible, it reminds us of Method acting, sort of.

It works like this. When confronted with an anti-Semite, or with someone who claims (or is sympathetic to someone who claims) that the Holocaust never happened:

1. Allow your immediate contempt and revulsion to express itself. Use verbal expressions such as, "Ugh. That's no good," and "Oh, please," and "*Feh*. They're animals."

2. Argue vehemently with others who disagree with you. Brook no protest. Tolerate no modifying observations.

3. Hint, or state outright, that "there is nothing to talk about," that "everyone knows what kind of person we're dealing with." Ignore the fact that, if everyone knew, no one would be arguing with you.

4. Bring the discussion to a close by refusing to engage in it anymore on the grounds that anyone who disagrees with you is naïve, idealistic, or has been "brainwashed."

It's that simple. Break up the rush-hour traffic jam, which is your normal intellectual functioning when it comes to "these people." Don't bother with the stop-and-go. Just drive off the highway and cut across the field to your destination—which is Your Opinion.

32

LET'S KEEP KOSHER, FINALLY!

Canceling your subscription to the Oyster of the Month Club and throwing out your copy of *Ribs! Ribs! Ribs!* are excellent ways to return to your Jewish roots. Just remember, though, that kosher is kosher—strictly speaking, that is. There are degrees, of course. Conservative Kosher (kosher at home, anything-goes when you eat out) and Reform Kosher (one set of plates for kosher, one set for Chinese).

If you play it Orthodox, though, then remember: no more pizza with pepperoni. No more medium (let alone rare) steak. No more Shrimp Étouffée, Shrimp in Lobster Sauce, or Shrimp-Anything-Else. No more Chicken Parmesan, Clams Casino, or yummy Grilled Pork Loin with Anise-Pepper Rub. And—although it may hurt to face the fact—no more Fried Owl, Roasted Swan, or Cajun Blackened Bat.

13: And these are they which ye shall have in abomination among the fowls; they shall not be eaten, they are an abomination: the eagle, and the ossifrage, and the ospray,

14: And the vulture, and the kite after his kind;

15: Every raven after his kind;

16: And the owl, and the night hawk, and the cuckow, and the hawk after his kind,

17: And the little owl, and the cormorant, and the great owl,

18: And the swan, and the pelican, and the gier eagle,

19: And the stork, the heron after her kind, and the lapwing, and the bat.

20: All fowls that creep, going upon all four, shall be an abomination unto you.

Leviticus 11: 13–20

You say, "Okay, fine, I can learn to live without Baked Cormorant." And you'll have to give up Surf and Turf even if "Surf" doesn't refer to a lobster tail but to a nice piece of fish, because it is forbidden to eat meat and fish together—at least according to some.

But can you live without cheeseburgers? Or Fried Chicken Dipped in Milk? Or a Pastrami-with-Coleslaw-and-Russian special?

The rules and regs of what constitutes a kosher (or *kasher*, fit, proper) diet are extensive and elaborate. Here they are now:

1. Certain animals are completely verboten. This includes their flesh, organs, eggs, and milk.

2. Of the animals that you can eat, the mammals and fowl must be killed in accordance with Jewish law.

3. All blood must be drained from the meat or broiled out of it before it is eaten. "Rare" is not only rare, it's nonexistent.

4. Certain parts of permitted animals may not be eaten.

5. Fruits and vegetables are allowed! But they must be inspected for bugs, which you might inadvertently eat, which are forbidden.

6. Meat (the flesh of birds and mammals) cannot be eaten with dairy. Eggs, fruits, vegetables, and grains can be eaten with either

meat or dairy. Opinions differ as to whether or not fish may be eaten with meat.

7. Utensils and dishes that have come into contact with meat may not be used with dairy, and vice versa. Utensils that have come into contact with nonkosher food may not be used with kosher food. This applies only where the contact occurred while the food was hot.

8. Grape products made by non-Jews may not be eaten. By this they don't mean grape Kool-Aid. They mean wine.

To what purpose were all these restrictions and taboos promulgated? And what's the point of them today?

"As a health measure," it is commonly thought—i.e., back when Leviticus was written (c. 550–400 BCE)—pork was *terefah* (forbidden; Yid. *trayf*), "unclean" and, therefore, unsafe to eat. The same is thought to be held true for shellfish, all those fowls noted above, and so on. "Don't eat that stork," you can imagine our forefathers saying. "You don't know where it's been."

The practices of proper kosher butchering of chicken and beef were, and still are, more hygienic than those of ancient, medieval, *and* modern meat sources. The *shochet* (ritual kosher butcher) examines every animal he kills for signs of disease, which is more than you can say about the giant meatpacking houses. And kosher meat is required to be eaten within a matter of days after its slaughter, which mitigates against the health problems associated with spoiled meat.

As for the prohibition of eating dairy with meat, or of using the same plates or utensils for both, there are rumors that "it's healthier that way," but they've never been confirmed. The reason for this taboo is, in fact, pretty straightforward: The Torah says you can't do it. *Thou shalt not seethe a kid in his mother's milk,* says Exodus 23:19, and the same thing is said two more times, in Exodus (34:26) and Deuteronomy (14:21).

And that, for devout Jews, is enough. The Torah doesn't give a reason for this rule, and they don't ask for one.

In fact, the entire "it's hygienic" rationale is a relatively recent gloss on one of the main purposes of *kashruth* (Orthodox rules for keeping kosher): to set the Jews apart from everyone around them—the "barbarians"—and especially the Greco-Roman world, in which pleasure and sensuality were highly prized.

Well. It worked for a few centuries, anyway.

Jews, in fact, were prohibited from buying wine, milk, and cheese from Gentiles (butter, for some reason, was allowed) and from eating bread that had been baked by Gentiles. The Talmud explains, "We should not eat their bread because we may be led thereby to drink their wine. We should not drink their wine because we may be led thereby to intermarry with them, and this will only lead us to worship their gods."

As in the children's book *If You Give a Mouse a Cookie*, one thing leads to another. If you let a Jew eat a muffin baked by a Gentile, pretty soon he'll be over at the Gentile's house, getting drunk and marrying the Gentile's daughter and worshipping Baal or Zeus or G-d knows what.

So there are your reasons for keeping kosher: a healthier, if more extremely limited, diet; and to set you apart from the barbarians and Gentiles (and the nonkosher Jews) who surround you.

And the thing is, it will work. So think about it and maybe give it a try. You can always fall (or jump) off the wagon if the lure of lasagna, lobster, or lamb korma becomes too much to resist.

33

DISCIPLINE YOUR SON THE OLD TESTAMENT WAY

It's easy to misconstrue the adage "Spare the rod and spoil the child." It seems to mean, "Don't hit your child with a rod. Spoil him instead."

But it doesn't mean that. It means, "*If you* spare the rod, *then you will end up* spoiling the child."

So don't spare the rod. Hit the child with the rod! Do it for the same reason we always inflict pain on people when they fail to behave according to our demands: for their own good.

Or, if that seems a bit severe, take a look at what the Torah has in mind for dealing with a disobedient son.

It presents its advice in the context of a universal situation, familiar to parents from sea to shining sea. But bear in mind that it was written several thousand years before any of our ancestors even knew of the existence of either the sea or the shining sea:

> *If a man have a stubborn and rebellious son, which will not obey the voice of his father, or the voice of his mother, and that, when they have chastened him, will not hearken unto them:*

Parents! Which of us hasn't been there? And in response, what do you do? Talk to him, at which point he simply says what he thinks you want to hear and otherwise squirms and evades like a trapped witness in a trial? Threaten to withhold privileges, which is a threat he is probably incapable of believing you would ever actually carry out? Ground him, condemning him to his hellish bedroom, with nothing for amusement except state-of-the-art audio, video-on-demand, and a souped-up computer connected to broadband?

Whatever you try, does it work?

If not, you've come to the right place. Now that you've read Deuteronomy 21:18, take a look at verses 19 and 20:

> 19: *Then shall his father and his mother lay hold on him, and bring him out unto the elders of his city, and unto the gate of his place;*
> 20: *And they shall say unto the elders of his city, This our son is stubborn and rebellious, he will not obey our voice; he is a glutton, and a drunkard.*

It may be hard to determine if your city actually has elders. And if it does, it's possible that they're merely creepy old men. But the no-nonsense crispness of this advice makes it worth putting up with a certain amount of elder creepiness.

Deuteronomy is quite clear as to what happens next:

> 21: *And all the men of his city shall stone him with stones, that he die: so shalt thou put evil away from among you; and all Israel shall hear, and fear.*

"All Israel" should be taken figuratively, and can mean "all Sherman Oaks," "all Chicago," "all Pikesville and northwest Baltimore," "all the Main Line and certain contiguous areas of Philadelphia," and so on.

Got that, stubborn and rebellious Jewish sons everywhere? You think having your cell-phone account ended hurts—try being stoned (with actual stones, wise guy) by all the men in town.

It wouldn't be fair to spring this exciting new technique in same-family juvenile penology upon your drunken, gluttonous offspring without warning. So make sure he knows the stakes involved and the

Disobedient son being stoned by elders of the village. Sometimes being pummeled to death by a fusillade of rocks is the only language certain children understand.

penalty he's risking with his bad behavior. Forget e-mail (they seem to ignore it), leaving little notes (he'll say he didn't see it), face-to-face verbal communication (he'll "forget"), or calling (he'll send you to voice mail and claim your message wasn't recorded). Try texting. They usually respond to that.

And if he protests with the usual defenses ("That isn't fair," "That's illegal," "You're crazy," etc.), make sure he reads Exodus 21:17:

And he that curseth his father, or his mother, shall surely be put to death.

"You've got to be kidding," he'll say. At that point, refer him to Leviticus 20:9:

For every one that curseth his father or his mother shall be surely put to death: he hath cursed his father or his mother; his blood shall be upon him.

Forget the rod. The rod is for wimps. This is Biblical child raising by people for whom an "energy drink" was ditch water and "video games" meant "hallucinating mirages on the desert while slowly dying of thirst." There's no better way to reignite your slumbering Old Testament patriarch. Your son gets a firm hand just when he needs it most, and you get to feel like George C. Scott in *The Bible.*

Oh, and a word about guilt. Of course you'll feel guilty about issuing these threats. You're supposed to. You're Jewish. But being lenient was what got you into this situation in the first place. So please, by all means, feel guilty. But do it anyway.

He'll thank you for it later.

34

How to Recognize a No-Goodnik

Remember no-goodniks? Even if you're too young or un-Jewish to know that the original Yiddish form of the word is *nishtgutnick*, (no-good person), you should know that the no-goodniks of old were rascals, layabouts, and cads who perpetrated shenanigans, did people dirt, and behaved badly.

People don't talk about no-goodniks these days. They talk about "scumbags" and "douchebags," and if they're especially stylish and up-to-date they might call someone a "douche." And that's a shame, because the range of human behavior (especially bad behavior) is much broader than can be encompassed by a bunch of —bags.

So expand your perception of what, and who, is out there. Forget the jerks and the dickwads and the pricks and the assholes. The more you can learn to think in terms of *mamzers* (bastards), *ganefs* (thieves, crooks), and *trombeniks* (bums, ne'er-do-wells), the more Jewish you'll be.

And for a real immersion into the Jewish tradition, try finding a no-goodnik. Here's a rough field guide to help you identify one:

1. He's not a *mensch.* He doesn't behave honorably, act unselfishly, or show concern for other people. He's not thoughtful, trustworthy, or mature.

2. He often is, to at least some extent, a *putz.* He's hurtful, self-ish, grabby, and oblivious of others. He treats people wrong. He uses. He takes advantage of. And he can be really smug, self-satisfied, and proud of himself when he does.

3. He is almost certainly a *ligner* (a liar). He lies to members of both sexes but he especially lies to, takes advantage of, and manipulates women.

4. He's probably not a woman. It's uncommon to hear of a lady no-goodnik. Yes, it's unfair. This is one more example of traditional Judaism's atavistic sexism and iffy treatment of half the Jewish, and human, race. In any case, while a woman can't be a no-goodnik, at least she can be a *kurveh* (whore, prostitute), a *shlooche* (slut), a

No-goodnik attempts to seduce woman by massaging her back with his ear.

chaleria (an evil woman), or a *yachneh* (a coarse, loud woman). Okay, they're almost all male-defined terms and they're all worse than being a rascal. But it's a start.

5. He can be a *shlepper* and even a *shnorrer.* That is, the no-goodnik can be a parasite, a sponger, a moocher, and a leech. He can also qualify as a *shtunk* (a lousy human being), a *bohmer* (bum), or a *groisser gornisht* (a big good-for-nothing).

You get the idea. Being a no-goodnik entails committing a lot of social sins and committing ethical, as opposed to legal, malfeasance. It's not quite like being a criminal (G-d forbid), but it's worse than being a *shmoe*, a *shnook*, or a *shmendrik*.

Now get out there and find one! And good luck, you *opnarer* (shady operator).

35

FRINGE BENEFITS: THE *TALLIT*

s everyone knows, Americans are slobs who will wear anything anywhere. People pay two hundred bucks a ticket for a Broadway show and arrive in overalls. Passengers file aboard transcontinental flights dressed in shorts, Peyton Manning jerseys, and flip-flops.

The idea of the public sphere as a shared space where we all create a common experience, where you make an effort to look nice for others because they're doing the same for you—forget it. It's *kaput*. You want that, go to Italy. Otherwise, stay here, stroll through any mall, behold the sweat suits and the baggy jeans and the T-shirts, and it dawns on you that, outside the office or the workplace, half the population would essentially rather walk around in pajamas.

That's why it will be all the more radical when, next time you go to a Reform synagogue, you a) wear a nice jacket and tie (if you're a man— although it would be really radical if you're a woman); and b) put on a *tallit*.

Or *tallis*. Either way, it's the prayer shawl, a rectangular scarf (or, if you're Orthodox, a robe) made of wool, silk, or linen, at either end of which are fringes called *tzitzit*. Most *tallitot* (pl.; also *talleisim*) have an embroidered strip along one edge, called the *atarah* (crown), which often displays the blessing one recites before putting the thing on.

If you've grown up Orthodox or Conservative, one of the most disorienting things about a Reform service is the sight of men *not* wearing prayer shawls. You feel like you're seeing something transgressively informal. It's like visiting the synagogue on the off-hours (to talk to the rabbi; to pick up kids at Hebrew school), when there's no service, and seeing people walking around and hanging out in the sanctuary as though it's just another auditorium.

Interestingly, though, while the *tallit* has for centuries been a worldwide symbol of Jewish attire, its use really isn't mentioned in the Torah. The only thing Jews are commanded to wear are the fringes, to remind them of G-d's laws. This is firmly, if somewhat bizarrely, commanded in Numbers 15: 37–41.

> *37: And the LORD spake unto Moses, saying,*
>
> *38: Speak unto the children of Israel, and bid them that they make them fringes in the borders of their garments throughout their generations, and that they put upon the fringe of the borders a ribband of blue:*
>
> *39: And it shall be unto you for a fringe, that ye may look upon it, and remember all the commandments of the LORD, and do them; and that ye seek not after your own heart and your own eyes, after which ye use to go a whoring:*
>
> *40: That ye may remember, and do all my commandments, and be holy unto your God.*
>
> *41: I am the LORD your God, which brought you out of the land of Egypt, to be your God: I am the LORD your God.*

How will wearing fringes keep you from going a whoring? Stop asking questions. The whole point of the *tallit* is that it display the *tzitzit*.

You will note that the commandment doesn't specify wearing fringes just at *shul*. In fact, until 70 CE, when the Second Temple was destroyed and the Diaspora outside Judea began, Jews wore them all day, everywhere. (Hasidim today still do, wearing a *tallit katan*, or "little *tallit*," under a shirt, with the *tzitzit* remaining visible.) However, once Jews dispersed throughout other societies, and anti-Semitic persecution grew in tandem with the spread of Christianity, the rabbis ruled that *tzitzit* need only be worn once a boy was Bar Mitzvah, and then only in synagogue. (Many *tallitot* also have black stripes, which symbolize the Jewish people's mourning for the Second Temple.)

Arms go inside. It's not a scarf.

The particular kind of Jewish macramé involved in tying the *tzitzit* requires there be a series of windings around the strands at each corner of the shawl in the pattern 7-8-11-13. You will be the opposite of surprised to learn that these numbers can be data-mined for multiple meanings, including:

1. Four corners = the number of letters in G-d's name.

2. *Gematria* (Jewish numerology; see chapter 45, "Learn the Kabbala") tells us that 7 + 8 = 15, for which the Hebrew is the letter

combination *yod hay*, the first two letters in G-d's famously mysterious four-letter name also known as the Tetragrammaton; 11 is written *vav hay*, the other two letters in the name; and 13 is equal to the
letters spelling *echad*, which means "one." Thus, the four windings
mean "G-d is one," the punch line of the Shema and the central tenet
of monotheism itself.

3. 7 + 8 + 11 = G-d's name, and 13 stands for the Thirteen Attributes of G-d.

And more.

Getting into It

Putting on the *tallit*, in sharp contrast to putting on *tefillin* (see chapter
25, "Chillin' and Illin' with *Tefillin*"), is fairly intuitive. You hold it out
before you, with the *atarah* along the top, and you recite the blessing
inscribed thereon, either aloud softly or even just to yourself.

בָּרוּךְ אַתָּה יְיָ אֱלֹהֵינוּ מֶלֶךְ הָעוֹלָם

אֲשֶׁר קִדְּשָׁנוּ בְּמִצְוֹתָיו וְצִוָּנוּ

לְהִתְעַטֵּף בַּצִּיצִית

BA-RUCH A-TA A-DO-NAI E-LO-HAY-NU ME-LECH
HA-O-LAM A-SHER KI-D'SHA-NU B'MITZ-VO-TAV
V-TZI-VA-NU L'HI-TA-TAYF BA-TZI-TZIT.

Kiss the final word of the prayer, and then kiss the first word—gently,
discreetly, not with loud, showy *mwah!* Then sweep the *tallit* around
you as you would a shawl or scarf, perhaps pausing under it for a moment
of private meditation. Adjust it comfortably. . . .

But beware. Many people think it is acceptable to wear the *tallit* with
arms *around* it, so its ends fall between the torso and the arms, like a

scarf. This is an error. One should wear it as a garment, with the arms within, like a European man-of-affairs who has draped his jacket over his shoulders. This, of course, exposes one to the hazard of the *tallit* falling off, revealing one's relaxed-fit jeans and LeBron James sweatshirt. And no one wants that.

That's why you can buy a set of clips that you attach to each side of the *tallit* to keep it on.

Usage tips: Don't take the *tallit* to the bathroom. It's not nice. If you take it off briefly (e.g., for a bathroom visit), you don't have to repeat the blessing.

To take it off, just take it off. You're thinking, "There must be some mistake. Isn't there a ritualized way of taking it off?" No. Just take it off, fold it up, and put in back into that velvet or velour bag until next time.

36

HOW TO SACRIFICE A LAMB
UNTO THE LORD

hat could be better for beefing up one's Jewishness? Obtain a bull, a ram, a lamb, or some other Biblical-type animal, and . . . you know . . . *kill it*, as an offering unto the Lord. Because isn't that what our Old Testament forefathers used to do?

A good place to start when conducting an animal sacrifice is Leviticus, chapter 1. Those who think they might want to sacrifice a bullock may begin with verses 5–9. But this, arguably, is unrealistic. It's hard to get your hands on a decent bullock these days—hell, it's hard just to find a good bullock man to call and ask if he has anything in stock.

A more practical option is a lamb. As set forth in verses 10–13, the process is fairly straightforward:

a. Obtain a male lamb without blemish.
b. Kill it "on the side of the altar northward before the LORD." Presumably this means on the north side of your synagogue's altar. Of course, it's unlikely that your synagogue actually has an altar. So

kill it outside the building, on the north side. The chapter doesn't specify the sort of knife, ax, or other implement to be used or how to use it, so feel free to use whatever lamb-killing apparatus you have in the house.

c. Get "the priests" to sprinkle the animal's blood around the altar. Again, your *shul* probably doesn't have an altar, and you probably don't have an actual *kohanim*-type "priest." So ask the rabbi to sprinkle some of the blood on the *bimah*. He (or she!) probably won't do it. But how will you know unless you ask?

d. Cut the carcass into pieces, separating the head and the fat.

e. Ask the rabbi to lay the head and the fat (in that order—and of the lamb, not of the rabbi) on the firewood upon the *bimah*. If—as will almost certainly be the case—your rabbi refuses to allow you to start an open sacrificial fire in the building, construct an altar outside.

f. Wash "the inwards" (i.e., the innards of the carcass) with water, and do the same with the legs.

g. Ask the rabbi to bring it all—head, fat, inwards, legs—to the altar and burn (i.e., roast) the whole thing.

And don't worry about the smoke, because, as the Torah confirms, "it is a burnt sacrifice, an offering made by fire, of a sweet savour unto the LORD."

But, before you jump in, there's something you should know—animal sacrifice is a sweet savor the LORD hasn't enjoyed for almost two thousand years. It turns out that our forebears didn't go around sacrificing lambs, sheep, bullocks, or goats as much as you might have thought.

Followers of all religions did take part in animal sacrifices for thousands of years prior to the Exodus from Egypt. For this reason, scholarly thinking goes, G-d allowed the Jews to continue the practice, because the Israelites automatically associated it with being religious.

But in Deuteronomy, G-d (via Moses) sets forth a complex series of rules that must be followed for a proper animal sacrifice, the foremost being that it must not be done by anyone other than a lineal descendent of Moses's older brother, Aaron, nor in any place except a temple sanctified to G-d—who, by the way, preferred penitence, prayer, meditation, and good deeds for the expiation of sins, rather than sacrifice.

That's why Jews have not sacrificed animals unto the Lord since 70 CE, when the Second Temple was destroyed. The First Temple, built by King Solomon and completed in 960 BCE, was the first official place designated by G-d for the offering of sacrifices. It was destroyed by the Babylonians in 586 BCE. The Second Temple was begun seventy years later. There was a brief period, during the Jewish War (132–135 CE), when the practice was revived, but when the war was lost it was discontinued, as it remains to this day.

In other words, until the Third Temple is built in Jerusalem prior to the coming of the Messiah—we should only live so long—the practice of animal sacrifice has been essentially discontinued.

If you're looking for a symbolic sort of "sacrifice" involving a Biblical creature, to at least approximate the ancient ritual, loin lamb chops are, what—thirteen dollars a pound? And leg of lamb is nice and can be reasonably priced.

Commercially available lamb has been preslaughtered for your convenience. But that doesn't mean you can't buy it *and sacrifice it by giving it to someone else.* And, since even in ancient times a sacrifice was cooked, you can expiate your sins with this easy, tasty recipe.

Sacrificial Roman Lamb

3 tbsp. olive oil
1½ lbs. leg of lamb, cut into bite-size pieces
1 tbsp. flour
1 large clove garlic, finely chopped
½ tsp. dried rosemary, or 1 sprig fresh

4–5 oil-packed anchovy fillets, chopped
salt
pepper
1 tbsp. white wine vinegar
1 qt. disposable plastic food container

1. Heat the oil over medium flame in a frying pan. Fry meat in batches until well browned.

2. Return all the meat to the pan and sprinkle with flour. Cook, stirring, until flour is cooked.

3. Add the garlic, rosemary, and anchovies. Season with salt and pepper and stir for 1 minute or until garlic is fragrant.

4. Add the vinegar, simmer for 30 seconds, then add 1 cup warm water. Bring to a simmer, then reduce the heat and partially cover. Simmer gently for 1 hour, stirring occasionally.

5. Let cool, then decant into food container.

6. Take to local food bank, soup kitchen, or homeless shelter. Donate.

7. And don't go around telling everyone and taking credit for it. The best kind of charity is the kind you don't do for applause.

37

So You Want to Have an Opinion About . . . CHRISTIANITY

Of course you do. And you should! And you probably already do. But will it help enhance your sense of *real* Jewishness?

It depends. If you think about Christianity in the modern way, you probably think along the following lines.

Contemporary Way to Think About Christianity

✡ It's touching, how they believe that Jesus was the Messiah, but please. He wasn't. Look around. There's your proof. Assuming Jesus actually existed, he was a religious revolutionary who said some important things, but that's it.

✡ Plus, the more modern historiography delves into what actually happened back then, the more the religion of Christianity is revealed as a system of dogma and power relations *invented by Peter.* Of course, all religions, as human institutions, are "invented," and their dogmas and bureaucratic structures are the creations of mere mortals. But if you're going to hold a convention and vote on which books are holy and which aren't, how divinely sanctioned can any of it be?

✡ What threatens the credibility of the whole thing are all the denominations. There are too many variations and subdivisions and sects. How true can any of it be if every one of a hundred splinter groups thinks every other one is wrong? There's Catholicism on the far right, and some mild, all-but-secular Protestant offshoot on the left, and ten billion churches in between—not to mention the offbeat ones like Seventh Day Adventists and Christian Scientists. Those parents, who pray instead of taking their children to the doctor—it's a crime. And what's with the Mormons? Are they Christian? Of course they are. What else can they be?

✡ There's also the whole Russian Orthodox and Greek Orthodox thing, and other variations. They're like Catholicism only with a different "pope."

✡ Do they really believe in Original Sin? That everyone is Bad until redeemed? Guilty until proven innocent? That seems like a religion that's dealing from a stacked deck. Jews believe in sin (although "sin" isn't a very Jewish word; it's a Christian word), but not as an inherent state of being. You atone when you do bad things, yes. But being born isn't one of them.

✡ They believe in Heaven, which is nice. In fact it's Christianity's biggest selling point. Jews don't get to have an afterlife in any literal, conscious, hey-I'm-dead-but-I'm-still-me-and-look-there's-my-dog-who-died-ten-years-ago sense. Christians do.

✡ Some of them, but fewer than believe in Heaven, believe in Hell. Is it any more silly than believing in Heaven? Good question.

✡ All of the above holds to the extent that to be Christian is not to also be anti-Semitic. If being Christian means you also believe that Jews killed Christ and are therefore damned, then *Gai tren zich*, which, we have it on good authority, is Yiddish for "Go fuck yourself."

✡ A lot of the most vocal, proselytizing, fervent, insane Americans today are Christians. Granted, their Christianity didn't make them

nuts; it provided a context and a means of expression for their nutti-
ness. And, of course, there are vocal, extremist Jews, too. Are there
Jewish zealots who take the Bible literally and are essentially Jewish
creationists? Probably. Because let's face it: There's everything out
there.

✡ So, in summation, Christianity is familiar, to the extent that it's
not Hinduism or Buddhism, and its god is G-d, although rendered
sort of schizophrenically, which is confusing. They can be nice, *men-
schy* people, and they can be a pain in the ass—just like Jews. But, in
the end, come on. Miracles? Virgin birth? The empty tomb means he
was *resurrected*? Sorry. No sale.

The above is an impressionistic summary of the modern, multicul-
tural, cosmopolitan, liberal, live-and-let-live opinion most non-extrem-
ist Jews (at least in the United States) have of Christianity today.

How, though, should one think about Christianity to bolster one's
sense of traditional Judaism? In brief: less subtly. Go from zero to giving
up in two seconds. Make a token effort to "understand," then throw up
your hands and shake your head. Like this.

More Traditional Way to Think About Christianity

✡ Look, who knows what they think, the crazy *goyim*, with the
Savior and the Redeeming? The only redeeming that means anything
is when you have enough books of Green Stamps.

✡ I'll tell you something that may surprise you. Jesus Christ was
Jewish! He was a Jew! From whatchamacallit. Nazareth. They all
were! The apostles with their epistles. All Jews. True story.

✡ Catholicism, please, it's not worth discussing. It's so *oppres-
sive*. Although confession, look, who doesn't like to get something
off his chest? And they can be lovely people. The Italians from the

neighborhood, very *hamishe*, very demonstrative. And, of course, great cooks, everybody acknowledges that. I can relate to that. Otherwise, the saints, the angels, the Virgin Mary—you want to know the truth? It's all theater. We have *Fiddler*, they have mass. (See chapter 6, "Learn to Embrace *Fiddler*.")

✡ Communion? No. I don't even want to tell you what I think. I don't even want to know what I think.

✡ Although if you want to know the truth, talk to them about when they were in school. About the nuns. The Jesuits, okay. A little discipline, a little rigor, fine. Very intelligent and great debaters. We could all use a little more rigor. But the things you hear—I'll tell you the truth: It's a kind of coercive magic. They're indoctrinating them into a system of magic—you say ten hail-thises or five holy-thats and all of a sudden you're pure? Everything is forgiven and you start over? *This does violence to the human mind.* And then they wonder why the boys become hoodlums and the girls turn into tramps?

✡ And the pope? Infallible, please. With that hat. Sitting in that palace with all that wealth, passing the plate and blessing the poor while protecting pedophiles and forcing their religious beliefs onto our political scene. It's a *shanda*.

✡ Protestants, on the other hand—sure, they soft-pedal it, it's more reasonable. You go to a Protestant church, you don't think, "Oy, what century am I in?" But where's the *ta'am*? Where's the vitality? Methodist, Lutheran, Presbyterian, it never ends. Episcopalians—that's Anglican but for over here, right? That whatshisname invented—Henry the Eighth? Let's you and me invent a religion. Why not?

✡ As for the evangelicals . . . I can't even talk about it. I mean the *meshugge* ones. The ones who take the Bible literally and watch those *mamzer* preachers on TV, those *ganefs* asking for money. And then one day they turn up in a motel room with some chippie, ask me if I'm surprised. Stupid, stupid people. With the faith handling and the snake healing. And "intelligent design," that's a laugh. With the cavemen riding around on dinosaurs before the Flood. Just tell me: How can people be so ignorant? In this day and age?

And so on. You're striving for a combination of dismissiveness, contempt, disbelief, and outrage—at least in private. In public, behave yourself and act like a mature human being, which means smile and tolerate and keep your opinions to yourself. The harder it is to do that, the more you'll know you're connecting with your Jewish roots.

Jesus of Nazareth visits a synagogue. Sadly, we have no contemporaneous accounts of his Bar Mitzvah.

38

WHAT ARE THOSE ICKY JEWISH DISHES
AND DO I HAVE TO EAT THEM?

very ethnic group (like every nation, region, and, for that matter, family) has its traditional foods and many of them possess odd, mysterious, or off-putting names. Of course, just because a name sounds weird (phonetically or etymologically) doesn't necessarily mean the dish it represents need be objectionable. "Little tongues and bivalve sauce" sounds barbaric and disgusting, but "Linguine con le Vongole" sounds better and "linguine and clam sauce" is lovely and delicious, albeit unkosher.

Jewish cooking has its share of distinctive dishes with ethnic names, many of which are familiar, ubiquitous, and unremarkable. No one is baffled by a bagel. You're familiar with matzoh, borscht, and seltzer? Big deal.

How about *derma*? Or *gribenes*? Those are the kinds of delicacies you'll have to study—and at least *taste*—to reawaken, if not entirely feed, your inner Traditional Jew. So let's get started. Here's a partial list.

Off-putting Traditional Jewish Foods

Name	Literal Translation	What It Is	What It's Used For
Cholent	SHUH-lent, SHO-lent, etc. From the French (!) *chaud* (warm) and *lent* (slow).	"Overnight stew." Meat and beans, chickpeas, spices, bouillon, water, etc. Also bulgur, barley, potatoes, eggs, whatever.	Made on Friday and allowed to cook slowly overnight so it's ready on the Sabbath—when, among the Orthodox, cooking is forbidden.
Farfel (see also Matzoh farfel)	FAR-fl—From Middle High German *varveln*: soup with pieces of egg noodles.	Small pieces of egg-and-flour noodles.	In soups or as a side dish.
Fliegel, the	FLIG-gl— Yiddish: bird's wing.	Chicken, duck, or goose wing.	Specifying fowl part. "Who wants the *fliegel*?"
Gefilte fish	Yiddish, from German *gefullte*: filled or stuffed.	Boned fish (usually carp and/or pike) combined with eggs, onions, flour/matzoh meal, stuffed back into the fish skin and poached, then chilled.	Appetizer; *parve* (neither dairy nor meat; edible with either); traditional Passover starter. "Jewish Sushi," "Jewshi," etc.

Name	Literal Translation	What It Is	What It's Used For
Gergle	?	The neck of the chicken.	You stuff it with, uh, stuffing, and it becomes a delicacy.
Gribenes (also Gribnitz)	GRIB-en-ess, or GRIB-nits—Yiddish: *gribenes,* scraps.	Chicken skin pieces fried in the process of flavoring rendered chicken fat.	Snack, heart-attack provocation. "Jewish pork rinds." Also used as flavoring in, e.g., chopped liver.
Hamentashen	Prob. Yiddish: *montaschen,* poppy seed–filled pouches. In Israel called Oznei Haman, "Haman's ears."	Three-cornered pastries filled with jelly, fruit, nuts, etc.	Traditional Purim treat symbolizing tricorn hat of Haman, defeated enemy of the Jews. Or, in Israel, apparently, his ears. Whatever.
Kasha varnishkes	Kasha = buckwheat groats; *varnishkes* = Yiddish bow-tie-shaped noodles.	Kasha cooked in egg, then boiled until soft, on bow-tie-shaped noodles.	"Jewish comfort food." (Although arguably all food is comfort food for Jews.)

(continued)

Name	Literal Translation	What It Is	What It's Used For
Kishke (or Kishka; also Derma)	Slavic: gut or intestine	In general, Eastern European sausage; among Jews, beef intestine stuffed with matzoh meal, chicken or beef fat, and spices.	"A delicacy."
Lokshen kugel	Yiddish: noodle pudding.	Sweet (or savory) baked pudding of noodles, sugar, cinnamon, raisins, cream, etc.	Side dish to meal, or dessert.
Matzoh farfel	See Farfel, page 166.	Little pieces of matzoh.	Soups, added at the table for thickness and crunch.
Mun	Rhymes with "Brun" in Brunhilde— prob. from German *mohn*: moon. Was and is used to create "moon cakes," originally to honor Diana,	Ground poppy seed paste.	Pastries, cakes, etc. WARNING: DO NOT EAT BEFORE URINE TEST. Results will test positive for heroin or opium use, since both are derivatives

Name	Literal Translation	What It Is	What It's Used For
	goddess of the moon. Poppy seeds are called "moon seeds" in Germany.		of the poppy. Of course, if you *have* been using heroin or opium, you might as well have all the *mun* you want, then claim the test shows that you like poppy-based pastries.
Pulke, the	PULL-keh or colloquially PULL-kee— German: thigh.	Thigh of chicken, duck, goose.	Specifying fowl part. "If you don't want the *fliegel*, do you want the *pulke*?"
Rugelach	ROOG-eh-lach, where first syllable rhymes with "boog" in boogie-woogie and last syllable has guttural "ch" as in Scottish . . . oh never mind— Yiddish, diminutive of Hebrew *roglit*: creeping vine.	Small, rolled-up, crescent-shaped cookies. Can be filled with nuts, cinnamon, raisins, chocolate, or *mun* (!).	Dessert, snacks. Note: Labor intensive. Typically made by son's mother to bring to son's wife (the ingrate) on any of the holidays on which wife deigns to invite her.

(continued)

Name	Literal Translation	What It Is	What It's Used For
Shmaltz	Modern German *schmalz*: cooking fat.	Rendered animal fat—can be goose or pig but in Jewish cooking generally used to mean rendered chicken fat.	Instead of butter: for frying, as a spread on bread. "Cooking with butter is for the *goyim*."
Tongue	English: tongue.	The cow's tongue, roasted and sliced.	Deli sandwiches.
Tsimmis	TZIM-iss— Yiddish.	Sweet carrot compote.	Side dish. Also slang for a complicated to-do—a "federal case."

39

THE *MITZVOT*

The Torah is the defining work of the Jewish people, a combination founding charter, Declaration of Independence, Constitution, official history, and legal code. But its laws are no mere statutes passed by legislators. They're commandments from *G-d*, okay?

The Hebrew word for "commandment" is *mitzvah,* and the plural is *mitzvot.* A boy, when he "is Bar Mitzvah," is "made a son of the commandment." A girl, when she is "Bat," is "made a daughter." The use of "Bar Mitzvah" as a verb ("He gets Bar Mitzvahed next April") or a noun ("His Bar Mitzvah in April was appalling") is a Yinglish adaptation of the term.

So far, so good.

From this, oddly, derives the Yiddish use of "a *mitzvah*" to mean "a good deed" or "a special favor." In other words, in a prime example of the inherently ironic nature of Yiddish, the term for something you are ordered by the Lord to do becomes a term for something you do voluntarily. Thus, e.g., "The last thing I needed was more magazines—it's not like I have time to read anyway—but Judy lost her job and started selling subscriptions, so I signed up for some. What can I tell you, it was a *mitzvah.*"

As for the original commandments, if you're congratulating yourself for being able to name "all ten of them," don't put that gold star on your chart just yet. There are actually 613. Maimonides, cited by no less an authority than Walter Sobchak in *The Big Lebowski* using the Hebrew acronym of his title and name (Rabbi Moshe ben Maimon) as "the Rambam," compiled the definitive list of them in the twelfth century according to a series of criteria that are not without controversy. For example:

- Should one count every commandment by G-d to an individual, or only to all of Israel?
- Should one count as a commandment any order, even if it could only be followed at one place and time? Or only those that can be followed at all places and at all times? (The latter was Maimonides's choice.)
- How should one count the commandments with multiple Do Nots—as one, or should each Do Not gets its own number?

Not everyone over the ages has agreed with the Rambam's rulings. Still, by general consensus, "the Law" consists of 613 *mitzvot*.

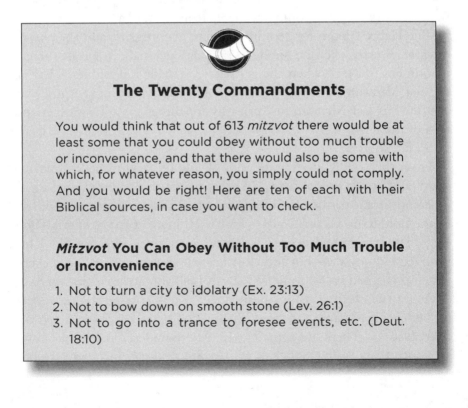

The Twenty Commandments

You would think that out of 613 *mitzvot* there would be at least some that you could obey without too much trouble or inconvenience, and that there would also be some with which, for whatever reason, you simply could not comply. And you would be right! Here are ten of each with their Biblical sources, in case you want to check.

Mitzvot You Can Obey Without Too Much Trouble or Inconvenience

1. Not to turn a city to idolatry (Ex. 23:13)
2. Not to bow down on smooth stone (Lev. 26:1)
3. Not to go into a trance to foresee events, etc. (Deut. 18:10)

4. A man must not remarry his ex-wife after she has married someone else (Deut. 24:4)
5. Not to have sexual relations with your father's brother's wife (Lev. 18:14)
6. Not to eat nonkosher flying insects (Deut. 14:19)
7. Not to crossbreed animals (Lev. 19:19)
8. Not to rob openly (Lev. 19:13)
9. Make a guardrail around flat roofs (Deut. 22:8)
10. Not to strike your father and mother (Ex. 21:15)

Mitzvot with Which, for Whatever Reason, You Probably Will Not Comply

1. Not to speak derogatorily of others (Lev. 19:16)
2. Not to take God's name in vain (Ex. 20:6)
3. To redeem the firstborn donkey by giving a lamb to a Kohen (Ex. 13:13)
4. To build a Temple (Ex. 25:8)
5. Wipe out the descendants of Amalek (Deut. 25:19)
6. To destroy idols and their accessories (Deut. 12:2)
7. Not to follow the whims of your heart or what your eyes see (Num. 15:39)
8. To set aside a portion of dough for a Kohen (Num. 15:20)
9. Conduct sales according to Torah law (Lev. 25:14)
10. Not to appear at the Temple without offerings (Deut. 16:16)

Of these, 365 are negative, while 248 are positive. And sure, you want to memorize and obey all of them. But slow down, because it won't be as arduous as you think.

For one thing, many of them can no longer be observed, thanks to the destruction of the Second Temple. So already we're down to a paltry seventy-seven negative and 214 positive, and even then there are bigger savings to come. Twenty-six can be obeyed only in Israel, and many by definition do not apply to women. That makes the final number more manageable but still leaves enough to assure that you live a righteous life.

Three categories of negative commandments are designated as yehareg ve'al ya'avor, *meaning "One should let himself be killed rather than violate it." Can you guess which three they are?*

1. Watching Fox News
2. Wearing underwear with holes
3. Going to someone's house for dinner empty-handed
4. Murder
5. Eating pastrami with mayo. Or salsa.
6. Idolatry
7. Not calling your mother
8. Forbidden sexual relations
9. Dating some hoodlum, or a musician
10. Choosing to vacation in Bora Bora or some other *goyische* place rather than finally visiting Israel

(Answers: 4, 6, 8)

Man happily, if unrighteously, violating Commandment No. 69 (*Men must not shave their beards with a razor, Lev. 19:27*).

40

HONOR THE SABBATH.
IT WOULDN'T KILL YOU.

on-Orthodox Jews take the Sabbath for granted, and think of it as a minor day-you're-supposed-to-go-to-*shul*-because-you-don't-go-to-school-or-probably-don't-go-to-work, but in fact Shabbat/the Sabbath/Saturday is one of the holiest days in the Jewish year. And it comes every week!

Of course, everyone knows that observing the Sabbath is number Four of the Ten Commandments. But unless you've read the whole text you might not know how comprehensive the commandment is. If you thought it was okay for you and your maidservant to rest but for your cattle to go about their business, forget it:

> *Remember the sabbath day, to keep it holy. Six days shalt thou labour, and do all thy work: But the seventh day is the sabbath of the LORD thy God: in it thou shalt not do any work, thou, nor thy son, nor thy daughter, thy manservant, nor thy maidservant, nor thy cattle, nor thy stranger that is within thy gates.*
>
> *Exodus 20:8–10*

In fact, the Mishnah—the first major redaction of the Oral Law accumulated over centuries, created in 200 CE—lists thirty-nine activities

that are prohibited on Shabbat. If you really want to renew your connection to Judaism, and issue a Torah-sanctioned "No!" to the hectic pace of today's multitasking world, just learn to refrain from all these for twenty-four hours once Friday evening rolls around.

Activities Prohibited on the Sabbath

1. Planting
2. Plowing
3. Reaping
4. Binding sheaves
5. Threshing
6. Winnowing
7. Selecting
8. Grinding
9. Sifting
10. Kneading
11. Baking
12. Shearing wool
13. Washing wool
14. Beating wool
15. Dyeing
16. Spinning
17. Weaving
18. Making two loops
19. Weaving at least two threads
20. Separating two threads
21. Tying
22. Untying
23. Sewing at least two stitches
24. Tearing for the purpose of sewing

25. Trapping
26. Slaughtering
27. Flaying
28. Salting meat
29. Curing hide
30. Scraping hide
31. Cutting hide into pieces
32. Writing two or more letters
33. Erasing
34. Building
35. Tearing something down
36. Extinguishing a fire
37. Igniting a fire
38. Applying the finishing touch
39. Transferring between domains

Doesn't just reading this list make you want to take an entire day off? Number 38 seems oddly nebulous, and the last one seems to have something to do with relocating your Web sites, but maybe it means something else.

The idea behind the Sabbath, say the devout, is to emulate G-d Himself, who famously rested on the seventh day after creating everything else in the previous six. G-d, of course, doesn't usually get tired, so if He needs to rest, how much more does mankind? The Sabbath, then, is G-d's gift to humanity.

Of course, modern life confronts us with tasks and temptations unimagined in the second century. Can you guess which of the following are not allowed on the Sabbath?

Things Commonly Done on the Sabbath Today

1. Staying in bed and having sex
2. Making coffee and breakfast
3. Taking a shower, shaving, getting dressed
4. Checking and replying to e-mail
5. Reading papers or magazines either on paper or online
6. Driving kids to various activities or friends' houses

7. Shopping
8. Going nuts trying to solve the *New York Times* Saturday crossword puzzle
9. Driving self to various places
10. Buying and preparing food
11. Listening to radios, MP3 players, and stereos
12. Operating toasters, ovens, microwaves, and coffeemakers (see number 2)
13. Walking/hiking dog(s)
14. Grooming, washing pets
15. Going to the movies or theater
16. Going to the beach/lake/pool and swimming
17. Playing sports or watching kids, others playing sports
18. Going to the hair salon
19. Doing home improvement projects and chores
20. Cleaning, vacuuming, doing laundry, etc.
21. Washing car(s)
22. Bicycling, skating, skiing, etc.
23. Gardening
24. Practicing musical instruments
25. Going to the gym/Pilates/etc. and working out
26. Strolling and window-shopping
27. Watching television
28. Working on hobbies
29. Fighting with boyfriend/girlfriend, spouse, children
30. Talking on the phone to parents, kids, friends, enemies, frenemies
31. Drinking, taking/smoking/"doing" drugs
32. Playing video games
33. Working thermostats, air conditioners, space heaters, and humidifiers
34. Turning electric lights on and off
35. Getting out of town for the day
36. Going to auctions
37. Applying the finishing touch
38. Transferring between domains

It's a trick question! None of them (with the possible exception of number 1) are allowed, according to the traditional rules of Sabbath observance.

Now, guess what these things, also usually not done on the Sabbath, have in common:

Other Things Not Commonly Done on the Sabbath

1. Lighting candles eighteen minutes before sundown on Friday evening and reciting special prayers
2. Serving a festive and celebratory Sabbath dinner
3. Going to synagogue Friday night and/or Saturday morning
4. Reading the holy books
5. Learning and discussing the Law
6. Enjoying a Sabbath feast at noon. (Assuming Orthodox services are finished by noon.) (See *Cholent* in chapter 38, "What Are Those Icky Jewish Dishes?")
7. Resting

What they have in common, of course, is the fact these are the only things you're *supposed* to do. Even walking beyond a certain distance, the rabbinically permitted "Sabbath limit" or *Techum Shabbat,* is verboten—even to synagogue, which is why the Orthodox live close to theirs. Forget driving.

Granted, devout Jews have found ways, over the centuries, to cheat and to expand the range of the permissible. They hire *Shabbos goyim,* i.e., Gentile helpers for the Sabbath, to turn the lights and the oven on and off at home (in the synagogue, too, probably) and perform other necessary tasks between sundown on Friday and Saturday nights. Orthodox communities have strung up wires on utility poles around their neighborhoods, which, when suitably blessed, delineate a larger area (an *erub*) in which they're allowed to walk.

But those are minor tweaks. During the Sabbath they don't do housework, homework, or work-work. They don't handle money or electricity or automobiles. They walk to synagogue, pray, and come home. Period. They detach themselves from life as we know it. No phones, computers, tweets, texts, snark, tunes, beats, "friends," pokes, chat, or mail. Once a week, they just stop. Talk about going it old-*shul*!

The list of activities forbidden on the Sabbath is extensive—and, as is everything in Jewish law, subject to debate.

A man starts to wonder if it's okay to have sex on the Sabbath. If sex is work, it's forbidden; if it's play, it's okay. So he asks the first expert he comes across—a priest.

The priest thinks about it and finally says, "My son, one of the main purposes of a Catholic marriage is procreation. It is a responsibility, and is therefore to be considered work. Thus sex is not permitted on Sundays."

The man thanks the priest but pretty soon asks himself, "What does a priest know about sex?" So he asks the next expert he comes across, which is a minister, who is married.

But the minister says essentially the same thing: Sex is for procreation, is a responsibility, and is therefore work, and not allowed on the Sabbath.

The man isn't crazy about that answer either, so he decides to ask an expert with thousands more years of tradition and wisdom than either of those two clergymen. He makes an appointment to talk to his rabbi.

The rabbi thinks a little, then nods and says, "Ah. It's obvious. Sex is play, and therefore is permitted."

The man says, "Okay, but Rabbi, why do you say it's play, when the priest and the minister say that it's work?"

"Believe me," the rabbi says, "if it were work, my wife would have the maid do it."

41

USE A SLING TO INCAPACITATE YOUR ENEMIES!

These days, the methods commonly available for dealing with one's enemies are familiar and few. You make fun of them online. You sue them. Maybe, in the realm of office politics, you engineer a complex and fiendish scheme to advance yourself and crush them utterly.

Why not expand your repertoire of hostile actions and take a cue from one of the most beloved folk tales of our ancient Jewish past? We speak, of course, of the story of David and Goliath.

As everyone knows, young shepherd David slew gigundo Philistine soldier Goliath by swinging a rock around in a strip of cloth and then loosing it in the big lug's direction. It worked like a charm and people have been talking about it ever since.

Think how exciting it would be to deal with your own adversaries in the same way.

Imagine the looks on the faces of your business rivals, romantic competitors, and the general jerks you have to deal with at the office or in school or in daily life, when you step up in front of them, reach into your shepherd's bag, pull out a smooth stone, and start whanging that thing around while maintaining fearless eye contact.

David holds aloft Goliath's head after stunning him with a sling and cutting it off. Note sword, bottom, which weighs more than David and head combined.

But before you start practicing your sling technique, there are a few things you may not know about both David and Goliath:

1. Goliath was uncircumcised. This doesn't necessarily mean he was a bad person, of course. But it's a useful ploy to raise the issue

with your enemy. You might try yelling at him, "Hey! Are you circumcised?" He probably won't be expecting such a question and you can exploit his momentary confusion. Don't worry about his answer (which may be a lie, anyway). You'll have ample opportunity to find out the truth later. Afterward.

2. Goliath was either 6 feet 7 inches, or 9 feet 6 inches. The discrepancy originated in varying Biblical translations and, since Hebrew letters are also numbers, a possible mistaken identification of one letter for another from version to version. In any case, don't worry if your foe is over 9 feet tall. A precedent has been established in your favor.

3. His armor weighed 125 pounds. The head of his spear alone weighed fifteen pounds. But so what! Your enemy probably will have neither armor nor spear.

So far, so good. But now things get tricky, because it isn't clear exactly how Goliath died. One version of I Samuel 17:48–50 describes David confronting the brute:

> 48: And it came to pass, when the Philistine arose, and came and drew nigh to meet David, that David hasted, and ran toward the army to meet the Philistine. 49: And David put his hand in his bag, and took thence a stone, and slang it, and smote the Philistine in his forehead, that the stone sunk into his forehead; and he fell upon his face to the earth. 50: So David prevailed over the Philistine with a sling and with a stone, and smote the Philistine, and slew him; but there was no sword in the hand of David.

That's the story as we've generally received it. But look at the King James version of the Old Testament and you'll see that the chapter goes on:

> 51: Therefore David ran, and stood upon the Philistine, and took his sword, and drew it out of the sheath thereof, and slew

him, and cut off his head therewith. And when the Philistines
saw their champion was dead, they fled.

One doesn't like to think of David decapitating the guy he so niftily
and cleanly felled with a single stone, does one?

Well, take heart. One doesn't have to. Modern scholars believe that
verses 51–58 were added after the "original" text (whatever that can
possibly mean when it comes to the Bible). So they discount 51–58,
which clears up some strange ambiguities, e.g., in verses 31–38, King
Saul meets David, talks to him, and even gives him some of his armor.
But in the (bogus!) verse 55, Saul asks Abner, his captain, who this
young whippersnapper is.

All of this may seem like vaguely academic Biblical historiography to
some, but remember that, when you do slay your enemies with a sling
and a stone, *you needn't also cut off their heads with their swords.*

So if some bystander challenges what you've done (by saying, e.g.,
"Hey, you forgot to cut off the dude's head, like David did in I Samuel
17:51"), just ignore it. That guy is a Biblical literalist and doesn't know
what he's talking about.

How to Use a Sling

The sling used by David is alternately shown as either a single uniform
strip of cloth, or a wider pouch of cloth somehow attached to two long,
narrower strips. The standard sling these days is based on the latter
model, and consists of a pouch at the center of two lengths of attached
cord. One benefit of using cord or twine is that you can fashion one end
into a slipknot, like that on a yo-yo, to easily loop around and anchor
on a finger.

Once that's done, fit the projectile (which should weigh between one
and two ounces) into the pouch and grasp the other lead in your palm.
Then choose between two slinging methods.

The first, which offers power at the expense of accuracy, calls for you
to swing your arm up from under, as though pitching underhanded in

softball. Wheel your arm once or twice like this, and then let go of the loose end of the cord as your arm becomes almost parallel to the ground. In this way you put the full force of your entire arm into the sling.

The other way, less powerful but more accurate, mimics the motion of a lasso or Argentine bolo. Swing the sling around the top of your head in a rotating motion from the elbow. Let go of the cord after two or three revolutions.

In both cases the sling should remain anchored to your finger. How David kept hold of his sling, which had no finger attachment, is unknown. Maybe he managed to grip the stationary end in the last three fingers of his hand, while releasing the other end by opening his index finger and thumb. Or maybe he just let go of the whole thing and kept an ample supply of slings on hand.

42

LET'S SUMMER IN THE CATSKILLS
IF THEY'RE STILL THERE

What's not to like? Food, huge swimming pools, golf, food, activities for the kids, walks amid "Nature," and with food, tennis, air-conditioned rooms, food, and, so you shouldn't go hungry, food. And then dessert, and then food.

The resorts' very names evoke hedonistic summer fun, miles from the baking city: the Concord, the Nevele, Kutsher's, Grossinger's, Brown's, Brickman's, the Gibber, the Pines, and more, all set in the actually-quite-beautiful Catskill Mountains northwest of New York City and southwest of Albany. They offer summer camp for families without the camp, a cruise ship's amenities without all that bothersome confinement on a boat and the ocean's potential to make you seasick.

Before the invention of air-conditioning, summers in New York were suffocating and unbearable for Jews. (They were also suffocating and unbearable for Christians, Muslims, Shintoists, atheists, and everybody else.) Rich families had begun fleeing to the Catskills as early as the nineteenth century; by the middle of the twentieth, the region was dotted with resort hotels, bungalow colonies, summer camps, camping grounds, and bed-and-breakfasts. How could it not be, when two hours away was a teeming metropolis of eight million people dying to get to someplace nice and cool?

Of course, many Jewish families had one requirement that other religious and ethnic groups didn't: They needed kosher meals. So a number of Jews-only resorts sprang up and flourished, offering outdoor fun by day and entertainment by night.

Thus, the Borscht Belt, a sort of petri dish for Jewish standup comedy, from which emerged Henny Youngman and Rodney Dangerfield and Milton Berle and Danny Kaye and Phyllis Diller and Jack Carter, Joan Rivers, Don Rickles, Woody Allen—enough? No?—Shecky Greene, Sid Caesar, Jackie Mason, Mel Brooks, and George Burns, and others AND JERRY LEWIS, *ya-heidle-floogle* with the joking and the *kibbitzing* and the running around and being a crazy person . . . thing.

Sure, you can go to Atlantic City (casinos, boardwalk, world-famous Atlantic Ocean), Ocean City (smaller, no casinos), and other points on the Jersey Shore. But nothing is or can be as Jewish as the Catskills. Let's see how the old resorts are doing.

Grossinger's Catskill Resort Hotel

Bad news: Grossinger's closed in 1986 and is now in what one source calls "a state of urban decay." As of 2009 only the golf course remained in use. This was the model for Kellerman's Mountain Resort, used as the setting for (the first) *Dirty Dancing*. There are, or were, or may be, plans—by the same company that has purchased the Concord and Kutsher's—to build a luxury boutique hotel on the golf course. We'll see.

The Concord

Good news and bad news.

First the good: As the Web site of the Concord Resort Hotel and Golf Club says, misplaced comma and all, "The Concord Resort & Golf Club, is the home of the World Famous 'Monster' Golf Course rated by *Golf Digest* as one of America's 100 Greatest Golf Courses."

The Web site also displays an artist's conception of a $500 million planned "four-star world class hotel" and a map of the proposed renovations. All this was unveiled in 2000, though, and in 2004 the Concord was sold to Empire Resorts, which also bought Grossinger's. Empire owns Monticello Raceway, site of a, uh, "racino." No, it's not a subatomic particle; it's a racecourse with a casino. Something similar is/may be planned for the Concord.

But the bad news is that, outside the golf course, the place is a mess. And, as if that weren't depressing enough, the facility is now used several times a year by the New York State Association of Fire Chiefs for live fire training. Then again, why not? It's big, it's relatively isolated, and it's got all that heavy Type-1 concrete construction. Who wouldn't want to practice on it by setting it on fire and putting it out and doing it over and over again?

Sure, Jews need a place where they can stuff themselves with prime rib and roasted potatoes and a million Parker House rolls and then run, *stampede*, through double doors to the dessert buffet. But firefighters need a place to train.

The Nevele

The Nevele—"eleven" spelled backward, reputedly to honor the eleven schoolteachers who, in the nineteenth century, first discovered the waterfall the hotel is named for—came, went, and then in the 1980s came back, redesigned with a neo-Deco look in hopes of luring Yuppie-era Jewish vacationers (and, especially, singles) back to the Catskills.

In 1997 it merged with the neighboring Fallsview Hotel and became the Nevele Grande Resort but, despite the appropriate retention of an "e" in "Grande," failed to make a go of it. It closed, and was scheduled to be auctioned off in September of 2009 when, at the, uh, eleventh hour, the entire site—buildings, nearly five hundred acres, and all—were mysteriously purchased by an unknown buyer.

The purchaser is not from the United States, and has enough cash to buy the place without a bank loan. What his (or her) plans are for the Nevele remains unknown as of this writing.

"Hi! Come on in! Do what we do, and walk in backward so your hair stays dry!"

The Pines

Buddy Hackett, Robert Goulet, and Tito Puente once played here, but today the Pines is synonymous not only with dilapidation, but with vandalism.

In August 2007, Heather Yakin of the *Times Herald-Record* (of the Hudson Valley) wrote: "The Pines resort is trashed . . . Over the past few years, vandals, arsonists and thieves stripped the old resort of its dignity. The Carleton staff building burned in 2003, the old day care went up in flames on July 20 and the Ritz staff quarters burned on Aug. 8. Thieves have stripped buildings of copper pipes and electrical wiring."

Lack of proper upkeep is one thing, but this is ridiculous. Talk about a *shanda* (a scandalous shame). It's a blessing that Robert Goulet didn't live to see it.

Kutsher's

This one is still in business. It was apparently bought in 2008 by the same developer who bought Grossinger's, and who wants to move the Monticello Raceway ("racino" and all) to the entertainment complex at the Concord, which he also bought. This would further solidify plans to make the Catskills a destination again, which would be good for all the hotels. It will certainly be a destination for this guy's creditors.

Kutsher's, meanwhile, was host to the American versions of the avant-garde, post-rock All Tomorrow's Parties festival for 2008 and 2009. The '09 lineup included the Jesus Lizard, the Flaming Lips, No Age, and others. An evening of nostalgic Jewish folk favorites and show tunes it wasn't.

The decline of the great Jewish Catskill resorts is sad, but perhaps inevitable. With assimilation, Jews began to forsake the traditional enclaves and swanned themselves off to Club Meds and Alaskan cruises and Hawaii, the Caribbean, and—of all places—Europe. Thank G-d they still go to Florida. It would be a shame to see an entire state go out of business.

43

BEYOND HIP, ALREADY: YIDDISH

We know you know what Yiddish is, and you have a sense of what some of its words and phrases mean. But why aren't you using it in your daily conversation?

Because it's archaic? It's old-fashioned and quaint and covered with cobwebs and reminds you of your grandparents and the weird smells in their homes when you visited for Passover? Sure, over the past fifteen years Yiddish has enjoyed a mushrooming of academic interest. But it's for studying, not for actually using.

It's hard to imagine pronouncing Yiddish words and expressions without also using a Yiddish-y intonation, and it's hard to imagine doing all that and not sounding like Henny Youngman or Jackie Mason. It's not sexy. It's the opposite of hip.

But that's its secret strength. Because guess what: Nothing, at this point, is hip. In the 1940s it was hip to be hep; in the 1950s it was hip to be hip; in the 1960s it was hip to be groovy; and in the 1980s it was hip to be square. But these days hipness itself is *mechuleh* (bankrupt). Why? Because the Internet now disseminates everything, immediately, to everyone, everywhere.

Talk about a Diaspora . . .

The newest cultural artifact—an expression, a piece of clothing, a style of music, etc.—goes around the world in an hour. The thing that young with-its in Williamsburg, Brooklyn, think is so knowing and esoteric at breakfast will be adopted and exhausted by twelve-year-olds in Djakarta by dinner. When everyone is with-it, hipness is out of business.

That's why learning and using Yiddish in your daily life can be so exciting. By doing so, you'll not only declare your independence from obsolete standards of hipness, you'll amp up your Jewishness big-time. So let's get started, *boobie* (honey).

Two people who probably speak at least some Yiddish.

So Nu? What Is It?

Yiddish is a form of German, written in Hebrew, incorporating bits of other languages such as Russian, Hebrew, and English. It was the language of the Ashkenazi Jews of Germany from around the tenth century and spread as they migrated to other countries—especially to America, which has the largest concentration of Ashkenazi Jews in the world. You know this? Good for you. Big shot.

The thing for you, as an Anglophone American, to remember is, while Yiddish when spoken in, say, Germany, is just another dialect, in the United States it is *inherently ironic.* In this country, anything you say in Yiddish automatically has at least two meanings. No. Three. It has at least three meanings.

For example, take the phrase *"Hak mir ein tchainik."* Its triple payload of meaning includes:

1. Its literal meaning. "Bang me a teakettle." Very onomatopoeic, if somewhat obscure, and limited in its daily applicability. Especially today, when so few people actually have teakettles and hardly anyone who does bangs it.

2. Its colloquial, "real" meaning. It means "to browbeat, to pester, to harangue." It can be used pejoratively, in protest ("Don't *hak mir ein tchainik* about the Springsteen tickets. If there are any left, we'll go. If not, not.") or pretend-neutrally ("Excuse me, that's my mother calling. Now I have to *hak her a tchainik* about getting her car serviced."). Note that bits of English can be substituted ("her" for *mir* and "a" for *ein*).

3. Its meta-meaning derived from the fact that it's Yiddish. By invoking this phrase, rather than using its English equivalent (e.g., "browbeat") you create an atmosphere of wry fatalism. You place the action or quality the Yiddish refers to within a larger context, one in which the foibles and imperfections of human nature are acknowledged, deemed more or less inevitable, and, therefore, are grudgingly tolerated. "Don't nag me" just means "Don't nag me." "Don't *hak me a tchainik*" means "I know why you feel you have to nag me, but I also know that *you* know why I don't want to be nagged, so do me a favor and don't nag me."

Neat, eh? *Vo den?* ("What else? What did you expect?") As with music, you can't just study this phenomenon and learn it by rote. You have to get a feel for it, too.

But that takes time. Meanwhile, study these words and phrases and learn them by rote. The feeling will come later, *alevei* ("It should only happen!").

A Short Lexicon of Basic Yiddish

a bisel—a little
Abi gezunt!—As long as you're healthy!
ahf tsores—in trouble
Alevei!—It should happen to me (to you)!
alter kocker—an old man or old woman
Ayn klaynigkeit!—Yeah, sure! (sarcastic)
baleboosteh—Mistress of the house. Used to mean a real homemaker, a great hostess.
bashert—fated or predestined ("They met when they were both in the emergency room. It's *bashert!*")
bentch—to bless; to recite a blessing
Bist meshugge?—Are you crazy?
boychik—young boy (term of endearment)
bubbe maisse—grandmother's tale (nonsense; old wives' tale; also, idiosyncrasy)
bupkis—(lit. beans) nothing; something totally worthless
chavver—friend
chazzer—a pig (a glutton)
Chub rachmones!—Have pity!
daven—pray
drek—excrement, feces; inferior merchandise; junk
ek velt—end of the world
emes—the real, serious truth
Enschultig meir.—Excuse me. Can be either sincere or sarcastic, depending on tone.
Es iz a shanda far di kinder!—It is a scandalous, appalling shame with regard to the children!
Ess gezunterhait.—Eat in good health.
farbissener—embittered; a bitter person; a sourpuss
farblondzhet—lost; bewildered; confused
farfolen—lost; disoriented
farklempt—too emotional to talk
farmisht—befuddled

farpitzed—dressed to the nines

farshnoshket—loaded; drunk

Farshtaist?—You understand?

fartik—finished; ready; complete

frailech—happy

fress—eat heartily; pig out

frum—pious; religious; devout

Gai avek!—Go away, scram!

ganef—crook; thief; burglar; swindler; racketeer

gelt—money

Genug iz genug!—Enough is enough!

gesheft—business (the whole *gesheft* = everything; the complete catastrophe)

Gevalt!—Heaven forbid!

glick—luck; bit of luck

gornisht—nothing

Gotteniu!—Oh G-d!

Halevei!—If only!

in miten drinen—in the middle of; suddenly

Kain ein horeh!—No Evil Eye!

kibbitz—to offer unsolicited advice as a spectator

klop—a real punch; a wallop

klotz or *klutz*—ungraceful, awkward, clumsy person; bungler

kuk—look. Give a *kuk.* = Check it out.

kvetch—whine; complain; whiner; a complainer

landsman—countryman; neighbor; fellow townsman from the "old country"

macher—big shot; a man with contacts

maiven—expert; connoisseur; authority

mamzer—bastard; "prick"

mazel tov—(lit. good luck) generally used to convey congratulations

megillah—long story

mekheye—extreme pleasure; delight

mensch—a "real" person; one who can be respected

meshpokha—extended family

meshugass—madness; insanity; craze

meshugge—crazy

meshuggeneh—crazy woman

meshuggener—crazy man

mieskeit—ugly thing or person

minyan—quorum of ten men necessary for holding public worship
(must be over thirteen years of age)

mitzvah—(lit. commandment) good deed

naches—joy; gratification, especially from children

nebbish—a nobody; simpleton; weakling; awkward person

nisht geferlech—not so bad; not too shabby. "I've seen worse."

nisht gut—not good; lousy

noch—yet (also, "on top of everything else," e.g. "He got into law
school—at Harvard, noch.")

nosh—snack

nosherie—snack food

Nu?—So? Well? What's new?

nudje—annoying person; badgerer

Oi vai iz mir!—O woe is me!

ongepatshket—cluttered; disordered; overdone

patsh—slap; smack on the cheek

pisher—male infant; a little squirt; a nobody

plotz—burst; explode

potchke—fool around or mess with

punim—face

pupik—navel; belly button

putz—slang word for "penis." Also used when describing someone
as being a jerk.

Reb—Mr.; Rabbi; title given to a learned and respected man

saichel—common sense; good sense; tact; diplomacy

shaigitz—non-Jewish boy; wild Jewish boy

shaineh maidel—pretty girl

shanda—shame or disgrace

shikseh—non-Jewish girl

shlemiel—clumsy bungler; an inept person; butter-fingered person;
dopey person

shlep—drag, carry, or haul, particularly unnecessary things, parcels, or baggage; undertake a tediously long journey

shlub—a jerk; a foolish, stupid, or unknowing person; second rate; inferior

shlump—careless dresser or untidy person; as a verb, to idle or lounge around

shmaltzy—sentimental; corny

shmatteh—rag; anything worthless

shmendrik—nincompoop; inept or indifferent person; same as *shlemiel*

shmoe or *shmo*—naïve person, one who is easy to deceive; a goof

shmooz or *shmuess*—chat; talk

shmuts—dirt; slime

shnook—patsy; sucker; person easy to impose upon

shnorrer—beggar who makes pretensions to respectability; sponger; parasite

shpatzir—a walk without a particular destination

shpiel—play (as in a performance)

shpilkes—pins and needles; on *shpilkes* = anxious

shtetl—village or small town (in the "old country")

shtik—piece; bit; a special bit of acting; a characteristic routine

shtup—push; shove; vulgarism for sexual intercourse

shtuss—a fuss; a to-do

shul—(lit. school) colloquial Yiddish for "synagogue"

shvantz—penis

shvitz—sweat; sweating

ta'am—taste; flavor; good taste; zest

Tahkeh!—Really! Is that so? Certainly!

toches—buttocks; behind; ass

Toches ahfen tish!—(lit., asses on the table) Put up or shut up! Let's get down to brass tacks.

trayf—forbidden food; impure; nonkosher

zaideh—grandfather

That should be enough to get you started.

44

HOW TO BUILD AN ARK
(Just in Case)

It is really, really important to know how to build an ark—especially for Jews. First, because of climate change: You never know when "global warming" will turn into "global flooding," and when it does, all of Christendom and Islam will run to the official account of the last time such a thing happened to see who is responsible. And who will they choose?

That's right. They'll blame the Jews (G-d forbid they should blame G-d), because the Flood for which Noah built the last major ark is described not in the New Testament, not in the Koran, and not in the Book of Mormon, but in the Old Testament. And since, in the basic reasoning of the world's great religions, Old Testament = the Jews, it will be considered their fault.

So this may be the place to suggest something that some may find surprising: *Noah wasn't Jewish.* We know this because a) he was a great sailor; b) he was history's first do-it-yourselfer and excelled in woodworking; and c) the first Jew was Abraham, who came ten generations after Noah.

Still, you should learn how to build an ark. Why? Three words: *Just in case.* As discussed in an earlier chapter, this is the general principle of practical Jewish pedagogy. "You're a jazz clarinet player? Fine—go to law school anyway. *Just in case.*" If there is another big flood, every

Jew will wish he or she had a big, capacious boat on which to escape the angry hordes.

And even if you think that global warming is no big deal—that at its worst it will only cause the waters of the seas to rise a measly few inches, perhaps getting a few beachgoers' ankles wet—that doesn't mean a major deluge cannot again be visited upon Man by the source of the original Flood: the Lord. G-d knows the preconditions for it are all in place.

The Flood of Noah's time came about, you will recall, because, according to Genesis 6:5–6, *GOD saw that the wickedness of man was great in the earth, and that every imagination of the thoughts of his heart was only evil continually. 6: And it repented the LORD that he had made man on the earth, and it grieved him at his heart.* This is what is known as "Creator's remorse."

Remember, though, that the purpose of Noah's ark was to assure the survival not only of Noah, his wife, their sons, and their wives (thus saving humanity itself), but of all the creatures of the land and of the air. Should we attempt to do the same with our ark(s)?

There is good news and bad news in this regard. First the bad: There are hundreds of thousands more species in existence today than existed in Noah's time—or, at least, we know of many more. The gathering together, in groups of two, of all 350,000 species of beetle alone promises to be a massive undertaking, even if you are assisted by your spouse, your children, their spouses, and their children. And you know how good children are at managing pets.

The good news, however, is that you no longer have to worry about rounding up the dinosaurs and herding them onto the ark, as our friends the Creationists believe Noah did. The dinosaurs may have provided cavemen six thousand years ago with a lot of useful transportation, companionship, and giant spare ribs, but today they're as dead as the dodo. So that's a consolation.

Let's call it a wash, then: Thousands more species to house, but no dinosaurs to take up all that room and possibly eat you, equals arks pretty much the same as the one Noah built and with which he attained such notable maritime, ecological, and humanity-saving success.

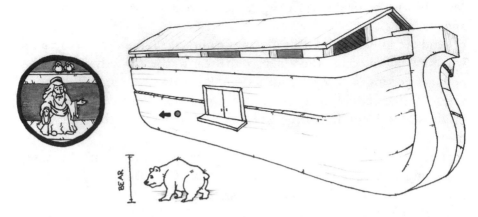

Design suggestion. Bear, included for scale, is not drawn to scale.

How?

The Bible says that Noah started with gopher wood. Interestingly, no one knows what that is. So if it's all the same, we'd rather use pine or cedar.

You can, if you wish, make the ark streamlined and ship shaped, although Scripture doesn't really specify that, and there are those who believe the ark "really" was more of a rectangular barge. It's up to you. And remember, there's nothing that says you can't use modern wood-working tools, nails, screws, drills, etc. You will, of course, have to line whatever wood you use with pitch, both inside and out, for waterproofing the vessel.

Concerning the ark's size, the Bible is explicit:

> *The length of the ark shall be three hundred cubits, the breadth of it fifty cubits, and the height of it thirty cubits. A window shalt thou make to the ark, and in a cubit shalt thou finish it above; and the door of the ark shalt thou set in the side thereof; with lower, second, and third stories shalt thou make it.*

Since one cubit equals 45.72 cm, or a little less than half a meter, the craft will be about 150 meters long, 25 wide, and 15 high, with three stories, a "window" (probably a ventilation space extending all around the top of the third story), and a door in the side.

As for the ark's actual construction, how hard can it be if a 480-year-old guy could do it without power tools? Just follow this simple step-by-step procedure:

1. Lay out the perimeter of the keel and affix its members to each other. Cover with pitch.
2. Fill in the interior of the keel with timber. Cover with pitch.
3. Build a first story, remembering to include a door in one side. The door should be fairly wide to accommodate the entry of large animals, but not dinosaurs. Cover all with pitch.
4. Roof over the first story, remembering to include a gap to which a stairway or gangway can be connected, so you and your spouse and your in-laws can move between decks. Cover all with pitch.
5. Build a second story. Cover with pitch.
6. Roof over the second story, also including a gap for a stairway or ramp. Cover with pitch in case it rains, which it damn well will.
7. Build a third story. Cover with pitch.
8. Build a roof over all, leaving a cubit-size ventilation slot all the way around. Cover all with pitch.

Once the ark is done, you may paint it in festive colors, in sober "battleship gray," or anything else. You'll need to apply several coats of primer to white out the pitch, or your colors won't "pop." Or, for a more authentic look, leave it (literally) pitch black.

Transport it to a lake or other large body of water for a test sail to make sure it's seaworthy. Be sure to bring aboard spare wood and pitch to patch any leaks that appear.

Then, for a more authentic experience, gather two of every living creature of the land and of the air, load in a lot of animal feed and your extended family, and wait for the rain.

45
LEARN THE KABBALA
(OR MAKE YOUR OWN!)

O r, okay, Cabala or, even better/weirder, Qabbala, all with the optional "h" at the end.

For those whose desire to reestablish a connection with traditional Judaism is matched by a desire for mysticism, numerology, and all-around kooky-on-stilts, the Kabbala is highly recommended. Although this is an overused colloquialism, in this case it really applies: Kabbala is Judaism on acid.

Say, for example, you wish to conjure up the devil. No problem. Here's a quote from *The Sword of Moses*, a tenth-century Kabbalistic book, which advises that the following incantation be written on a laurel leaf:

> *I conjure you, Prince whose name is Abraksas, in the name of SLGYY HVH YH GUTYUS HVH AFRNUHH HVH ASGNUHH HVN BTNUSYY HVH, that you come and reveal to me all that I will ask of you, and do not delay!*

The final clause indicates to the demon that you really mean it. "No, not when you get to the next commercial. NOW."

So yes, for a full immersion in Judaism's answer to the things written about by Dan Brown (and Umberto Eco), join Madonna—if she's still into it. Who can keep up?—and devote hours and hours to the study of this elaborate and endless form of Gnosticism-gone-gnuts.

What It Is

The Kabbala (or just "Kabbala" without the "the"), a series of books and practices that evolved over centuries, embodies what one might call the wild-and-crazy half of the Jewish religious character. On the one hand, Judaism has always been devoted to rationality, as embodied in the Talmud, and its use of logic, analysis, and (endless) debate to apprehend G-d—or, at least, to figure out what G-d intends for and wants from us.

On the other, as embodied in the primary Kabbalistic books *Sefer Yetzirah* (The Book of Creation), the *Bahir* (Brilliance), and the *Zohar* (Splendor), as well as countless lesser works, you've got your mysticism, with its irrational beliefs, incantatory rites, mumbo-jumboid fantasies, and numerological explorations of letters and words, all in an effort to get beyond the merely visible and to connect with the hidden essence of life, the soul, and the Lord.

You can't blame generations of Jews in the early centuries, in Asia, Africa, and Europe, for being attracted to the magical. You would be, too, if your community were persecuted, hounded, and denied many means of survival. Add to that the generally primitive state of human understanding of nature, and marinate it all in a broth of prior mystical traditions from the ancient Egyptians, Chaldeans, Babylonian-Persians, and Hindus, and the Kabbala's brand of Jewish pantheism–lite feels right. After all, since everything was made by G-d, why couldn't everything, one way or another, offer a way *to* G-d?

Besides, once you believe in the existence of G-d(s) at all—invisible, omnipresent, eternal, omnipotent, omniscient, remote, etc.—it's not that great a leap to believe that *everything*, including the alphabet, harbors a secret, unseen, superior meaning, available only to the ultra-wise or the truly gifted. One man's mysticism is another man's religious faith, and vice versa.

Even the most ardent believer yearns for some kind of certainty, and that's where numbers prove so appealing. Numerology—assigning numerical values to letters, and then doing esoteric mathematical operations on sacred texts to tease out their "real" meanings—goes back millennia; it was old hat by the time Pythagoras took it mainstream in Greek intellectual circles, and that was in the sixth century BCE. The Jews adopted the Greek-Hebrew hybrid word *gematria* to refer to Kabbalistic numerology.

Or you can skip the numbers and stick with the letters. For example, the "secret" name of G-d (the *Shem-ha-Meforash*) is, with regard to its proper spelling and pronunciation, a subject of extensive discussion. In the Hebrew Bible, the Lord's name is rendered in the Hebrew letters *yod, he, vav, he* (YHVH in English), but the holy name isn't pronounced; instead, in the manner that has baffled generations of Hebrew school students, one says, *Adonai* (My Lord). What if, the medieval Kabbalists theorized, Jesus of Nazareth was able to walk on water and

Dreidl—"G-d's Toy"

perform his other reputed miracles because he had learned the "secret" name of G-d?

Thus the Tetragrammaton, the four-letter YHVH, became the Kabbalists' equivalent of the philosopher's stone. A "wonder-working book" of the tenth century advised anyone who wished to walk upon water "without wetting his feet" to write (upon a plate of lead) this formula, in which the Tetragrammaton was rearranged:

HBKSHFHYAL	YHVHH	ASRGHYAL	YHVHH
HZASNHYAL	YHVHH	MUDDGHYAL	YHVHH

It's hard to find a plate of lead when you really need one, which might explain why so few people are strolling on Lake Huron.

Create Your Own Kabbala

This is difficult, complex material. Of course, the experts have no sympathy for the hapless Kabbala student. Rabbi Shul Schneerson of Lubavitch insisted that the study of Kabbala was a prerequisite *just for being a normal-type individual*: "A person who is capable of comprehending the *Seder hishtalshelus* (Kabbalistic secrets concerning the higher spiritual spheres)—and fails to do so—cannot be considered a human being."

Ouch. Then again, easy for him to say—he was great-grandfather of the Rebbe, Menachem Mendel Schneerson, who led the Lubavitchers in our time and died in 1994. So Reb Shul already had a job, and a congregation, and a sect, and etc., back in 1834–1882.

If the prospect of cracking such mind-roasting books as *Sefer Raziel HaMalakh*, Gershom Scholem's *Jewish Gnosticism, Merkabah Mysticism, and the Talmudic Tradition,* or Elliot Wolfson's *Language, Eros, Being: Kabbalistic Hermeneutics and Poetic Imagination* seems too much, you can cobble together your own pseudo-Kabbala and have almost as burningly abstract and sort-of-transcendent an experience as you'd get from studying the real thing.

For example, behold this abstruse yet plausible formula:

The dreidl is the Toy of G-d, as its most commonly used form embodies the Three Principle Polygons: the Cylinder that is its stem, the Cube that is its body, and the Cone that leads, as does a vortex, down to its Point, which is infinite in its absence of dimension and yet is that very Thing on which the object spins and, in so doing, defies gravity.

Cool, huh? It's completely made up. Sure, there are a thousand Web sites on the Internet that do just this sort of thing *and mean it*, every day. But why use theirs when you can create your own? Here's how:

1. Take something. Anything. A pencil. Okay, a tomato. Just take something. No, forget the pencil. Go with the tomato.
2. Get excited about its most general qualities and write about them in urgent, but general, terms.
3. Show connections between the thing you've chosen and something spiritual. (In the example below, the general terms you are to get excited about are written in all caps. The spiritual phenomena to which they are connected are underlined.)

EXAMPLE: "The tomato, with its NAME CONSISTING OF SIX LETTERS, reminds us of the six letters in *ADONAI*. Similarly, its THREE SYLLABLES replicate the three syllables of the Holy Name. The LETTERS OF ITS NAME, which secretly contain the words TOOT, MA, conceal an allusion both to the holy resonant sounds of the *shofar*, and to the proper deference to the Mother of the family who, indeed, is probably the person most often making use of the tomato in the familial setting. The AMBIGUITY attached to the tomato—it is A FRUIT, technically, but is more often employed as A VEGETABLE—embodies the All-In-One that is the essential Unity of the Lord.

"Further, its NUMEROLOGICAL PROFILE, according to the Basic Alpha-Numeric Cypher Attributes, is: 20-15-13-1-20-15.

Several facts immediately strike us with regard to this array. Prominently displayed is the 1, which announces <u>the eternal identity and indissoluble unity of HaShem and is central to the Shema</u>. Its *gematriatic* total = 84. Thus, its average *gematriatic* value = 84/6 = 14 = N. N is the first letter of NAPLES, A CITY IN SOUTHERN ITALY CLOSELY IDENTIFIED WITH THE USE OF THE TOMATO. N also reminds us of the <u>Book of Numbers, Fourth of the Five Books of Moses</u> . . ."

You get the idea.

4. Suggest, therefore, that the tomato is (select any three):
   a. holy
   b. sacred
   c. a key to inner wisdom
   d. the "fruit of the soul"
   e. The Two-Faceted Fruit-Vegetable of Gan Eden

Do this fifty, sixty times. Print out. Bind. Cherish, study, and suggest to all your friends and relatives that if they don't apply themselves to learning this, they cannot be considered a human being. Who knows? Maybe they'll buy it.

Tomato. Its Kabbalistic significance can scarcely be overstated, sort of.

46

How to Pack for a Week in Florida

hile non-Jews pride themselves on being able to fit everything they need for a week into one carry-on, Jews tend to take a different route. To them, packing involves taking everything they will need, plus what they think they *may* need, and what they think *you* might need, for a week. Note, however, that in this case "a week" means "for all eternity," because there's always a chance that wherever they're going, they will die there.

By way of example, peruse the standard inventory for a Jewish woman, from New York, packing to go on a seven-day vacation to Miami. Items are listed along with the rationale for their inclusion.

Sample Packing Inventory: Female

  4 bathing suits—because what if one doesn't completely dry overnight?
  5 cover-ups—because, even though you'll be sitting poolside or on the beach, G-d forbid your arms and legs be exposed to the sun
  5 outfits to wear during the day—in case you're not in the mood to lie by the pool or on the beach
  5 outfits to wear out to dinner

2 heavy-duty sweaters—in case the weather is bad or the buildings too air-conditioned

10 pairs of underwear

1 raincoat—in case it rains

4 pairs of pajamas—two very nice pairs to wear when room service is delivered; the other two don't have to be special, but you can't wear one pair for a whole week

2 bathrobes—one suitable for wearing "in public," i.e., for going down to the ice machine in the hall; one that no one will see you in

3 pairs of white pants of different weights

3 pairs of black pants of different weights

3 skirts—in case you "go somewhere nice"

3 dresses—in case you "go somewhere really nice"

3-4 different pairs of sweat suits—for when you don't want to be seen in public being *fully* casual and yet you are ready to be seen in public

5 books—because you never know what you'll be in the mood to read at the pool or on the beach

10 magazines—in case you're not in the mood to get into a new book because, after all, you're sitting by the pool or on the beach

A complete range of full-size bottles and jars of toiletries because you refuse to pay for those little trial or travel-size rip-offs

Over-the-counter medicines and first-aid supplies

Prescription drugs—all of them, but in a carry-on bag, because what if your suitcase gets sent to Tulsa or Guam?

Food for the plane—because you'll be G-d damned if you're going to pay six dollars for one of their *farkakteh* sandwiches

Food for the hotel room—to *nosh* on so you don't gorge at meals

Portable radio—in case there's a power outage or a national emergency

Extra cell phone, extra charger for your regular cell phone, and extra charger for the extra cell phone—in case child or grandchild calls, or someone calls with news of disaster befalling child, grandchild, or anyone else

Strategic Air Command Bomber Crew Emergency Necessity Kit, including water purification pills, pain-relief syringe, two hundred

dollars in euros, roubles, yen, and dinars, and chocolate bars, con-
doms, and cyanide capsule—in case "something happens"
List of emergency contacts, record of blood type, allergies, organ-
donor preference, and DNR instructions, and will or living will—
because you never know. It's a crazy world full of lunatics and
who-knows-what.

Part of essential matériel for trip to Florida. Not shown:
three tons of other stuff.

47

RAISE YOUR DAUGHTERS THE OLD TESTAMENT WAY

I n "Discipline Your Son the O.T. Way" you learned certain laws promulgated in the Torah that might, just *might*, prove helpful both in raising your drunken glutton of a son and in reinvigorating your sense of tribal tradition. But what if you need some sage advice about raising a daughter?

No problem. The Pentateuch is studded with cautionary tales, exemplary scenarios, and unambiguous laws regarding the proper behavior of a father toward his daughter. Mothers, alas, aren't mentioned much. So moms, you'll have to consult with the girl's father. But as the patriarch and head of the family, he knows better anyway, while your judgment is understandably clouded by the fact that you and your daughter are both girls.

As mentioned in chapter 33, about raising sons, there is no need to implement the actions described below. Instead, use them as child-raising tools. When your daughter displays behaviors to which you object, or just looks like she might, draw her attention to the following. Imagine how fascinated your daughter will be to learn that, as far as precedents in the Torah are concerned:

• **You can give her away.** In Genesis 19:8 we read how Lot, resident of Sodom, invited two men—okay, two angels—into his home as guests. Shortly afterward, a crowd of men swarmed the house and demanded Lot produce the visitors, so that the mob might know them. Lot, aware of the responsibilities of a proper host, refused. But, just so the group didn't go away empty-handed (as it were) and so the evening shouldn't be a total loss, he said, *"I have two daughters which have not known man; let me, I pray you, bring them out unto you, and do ye to them as is good in your eyes."*

It never, thank G-d, came to that. The crowd wasn't interested in the daughters and grew surly, but the angels made them blind. Then some other stuff happened, including a) the angels hustled Lot, his wife, and the daughters out of Sodom; b) Sodom was destroyed by fire and brimstone; c) Lot's wife disobeyed the command to not look back, and turned into a pillar of salt; d) Lot and the girls fled to Zoar but from there to a cave; e) the daughters, believing Lot to be the only surviving man on earth, got him drunk over two nights and had sex with him, to propagate the race.

Let's ignore that last part. Still, let your daughter know that if she doesn't straighten out, you can hand her over to an unruly mob. If she still doubts it, refer her to Judges 19: 16–30, where a similar scenario (man hosts guest, who arrives with his own concubine; crowd demands to know guest; man refuses but offers daughter) unfolds: *"Behold, here is my daughter a maiden, and his concubine; them I will bring out now, and humble ye them, and do with them what seemeth good unto you: but unto this man do not so vile a thing."* The text goes on to state that the man withheld his daughter, but did hand over his guest's concubine, whom the crowd "abused." Strong language, for the Bible.

If your girl still insists on misbehaving, inform her that:

• **You can sell her.** As a slave. So says Exodus 21:7: *And if a man sell his daughter to be a maidservant, she shall not go out as the menservants do.* Apparently this means that, while male slaves were given their freedom after six years, female slaves were kept in slavery forever. That's job security, Old Testament–style.

• **You can, in effect, rent her out.** Exodus 22:16–17 explains that, if your daughter is seduced by a man and thus loses her virginity, the offended party is you, as the property owner. She will be expected to marry her seducer, but only with your permission. If you refuse permission, the seducer is required to pay you "according to the dowry of virgins." In other words, since she will no longer fetch a virgin's dowry on the open marriage market, the seducer is required to "make whole" the father and compensate him for his loss.

If she protests, tell her that:

• **You can overrule her.** This, according to Numbers 30. Even in so serious a matter as a vow she has taken. A man's vow cannot

Wild, unruly daughters. Note musical instruments, which contribute to wildness and unruliness.

be altered by anyone. A woman's vow, however, can be cancelled by either her father or her husband. Granted, the father or husband has to overrule the vow as soon as it is made; you can't let it stand, or be told about it the next day, and only then register a complaint. It's an outrage, really, but that's how things were back then.

Finally, if all else fails:

• **You can escape embarrassment if she is not a virgin before she is married by having her stoned to death.** True, this entails finding out from her if she *is* a virgin—a conversation many fathers are not eager to have. But do it anyway, because she's your property, and it's for her own good. And take some comfort from this fact: As an object of stoning, she faces a penalty identical to that of the unruly son. So, see? In the end, everyone gets treated equally.

48

THE *MIKVAH*: COME ON IN!
THE WATER'S PURE.

Ever since the first time a caveman (or -woman) saw a watering hole and thought, "Hmm. I'm not very thirsty, but I wonder what it would be like to jump into that," humans have plunged into bodies of water for a number of different purposes, including recreation, pursuing fish, cooling off, and, of course, cleaning up.

But perhaps the most exalted use of water—aside from, you know, *drinking*—has been for religious ritual. The Christians have baptism. The Hindus wash before praying and, although there's no formal ceremony connected with it, bathe in the Ganges. The Muslims perform ablutions before prayer, too. Jews conduct a hand-washing ceremony before meals (most notably at the Passover *seder*).

And then there's the *mikvah* (pool), the ritual bath that has been a central element in Orthodox Jewish life since time literally immemorial. If you're a Jewish woman, availing yourself of this procedure is a way to really reinforce not only your flagging sense of Jewishness in general, but, specifically, your sense of Jewessness.

Let's get the most touchy aspect of it out of the way now: The central purpose of the *mikvah* is the repurification of a woman after her period.

Yes, yes, it's true: The idea of a woman *needing* "repurification" is offensive and primitive and insulting and patriarchal. To make matters worse, the use of the *mikvah* is not necessarily limited to women.

In fact . . . well . . . it so happens that new pots, dishes, and cooking utensils are immersed in its waters to consecrate them for use in the kitchen.

Now, you can find that objectionable, and no one would blame you. After all, you don't have to be a militant feminist to think of yourself as residing on a higher plane than, and being more important than, a ladle. So if it makes you feel any better, bear in mind that men, too, dip into the *mikvah*, although these uses are customary, not mandated: a groom on his wedding day; every man before Yom Kippur. The only required use of the *mikvah* by a man is on the occasion of conversion.

But for a woman, if she is so inclined, the *mikvah* can be seen as a means of reattaining a state of purity unavailable to men.

All right, don't jump in just yet. Let's go over the basics and then you can decide.

When and Why

The purification of the menstruant woman is not only a nice thing, it is a necessary and holy thing; a woman must be repurified or otherwise renewed after her menses, because from the beginning of her period to seven days after it ends, she and her husband are forbidden to have sexual relations.

This enforced separation can be seen as a superstitious inconvenience, of course. But it can also be regarded as a marriage counselor's stroke of genius, since the one thing guaranteed to make a man desire his wife even if he doesn't particularly *like* her anymore is the fact that he's not allowed to touch her. Literally.

The immersion in the *mikvah* brings that period of enforced separation to a formal, ritualistic end.

What It Isn't and Is

Contrary to what you might assume, the purpose of the *mikvah* is not, repeat *not*, to get you clean. You are required to be clean before you step into it, and the *mikvahs* in Jewish communities all offer showers, shampoos, etc., etc., to be used beforehand.

Second, it can't be a container of water added on to an existing structure, like a bathtub or a Jacuzzi. It has to be constructed as an integral part of the building or built into the ground.

Third, while those of us from Conservative, Reform, and further-left backgrounds are used to barely thinking about the *mikvah* at all, and even then consider it a sort of ultra-*frum* extra-credit type of thing, it turns out that a congregation is permitted to sell its actual Torah and its very synagogue, if the funds are needed for the construction of a *mikvah*.

That sounds weird until you realize that, without one, Orthodox couples would be forbidden to have sex after the wife's first period. And nobody would benefit from that—not the husband, not the wife, not the community, to the extent that there even *is* a community, since in such a scenario procreation (one of the first *mitzvot* [commandments], after all) would be, by definition, impossible.

Young woman newly purified by *mikvah*. Expression of dawning joy indicates she knows exactly what she is now able to resume doing.

The *mikvah* must be filled with rainwater. Seriously. There must be at least two hundred gallons of water, all gathered and siphoned into the bath according to a lot of very specific rules and regulations. If gathering rainwater is not practical, then water derived from melted snow or ice from a natural source can be used, and its transport from its source is also highly regulated.

Actually, though, you're not necessarily stepping (down a staircase) into literal rainwater. Most *mikvahs* consist of two or three pools. The original, consecrating rainwater is kept in one chamber, while the other(s) is/are periodically filled with tap water, and is/are rendered acceptable by a connection to and infiltration by the original cache of water. Contemporary *mikvahs* also have modern filtration and heating equipment to keep the bath a pleasant temperature. The depth of the water is customarily chest high.

Benefit Without Taking the Plunge

Before you throw this book aside and hurry off to the nearest *mikvah* in a sudden explosion of post-menstrual piety and zeal, bear in mind that:

- You don't have to be Orthodox to take part.
- Every city where there's even a small Jewish population probably has at least one *mikvah*. You can find them online.
- It's entirely confidential. Maybe the attendant knows you've come, okay. But otherwise, it's not like a health club, where you do it in front of a long picture window while pedestrians watch from the sidewalk and wave.
- It's clean, it's nice, it's pleasant. Maybe in the old days *mikvahs* were dingy and depressing. Nowadays, forget it. Who wants to suffer?

However, say you're just not interested in taking a ritual Jewish bath. Is there any way to apply the lessons of the *mikvah* to your daily life, to import old-fashioned Jewish practices and ideas into your smarty-pants contemporary life?

Yes! *Apply the menstrual taboo.* Make it a rule, with husband or boy-friend, that there be no sex from the onset of your period to seven days after it ends. Of course, if that threatens to subvert your plans to conceive, then you have bigger reproductive fish to fry, and never mind.

But if not, think about it. It's the *mikvah* principle without the actual bath (although you can, of course, symbolically repurify yourself in a more convenient bath, shower, Jacuzzi, etc., when the interval of denial is over).

The idea is not to declare yourself "impure." It's to provide some challenges and obstacles to your sex life in order to enhance its appeal and jazz things up. And if he doesn't like it, good. He's not supposed to.

49

INTRODUCTION TO THE *SHOFAR*

The *shofar* is the animal horn, usually that of a ram, used in Rosh Hashanah and Yom Kippur services. Its purpose is to remind us of Abraham's fidelity to G-d: While preparing, per the Lord's instruction, to sacrifice his only son, Isaac, Abraham was permitted, at the last second, to slaughter a ram instead.

Shofar. Has range to play almost all of "A Night in Tunisia."

You blow the *shofar* the same way you play a brass instrument (trumpet, trombone, etc.). The blower presses the lips up to the tapered end of the instrument and vibrates them quickly; the resulting buzzing sound creates a standing wave in the column of air in the horn, which is transformed by the shape and material of the horn into a musical tone.

To learn this is to think, for the first time, "Oh, I get it. This is why trumpets, cornets, and bugles are called 'horns.' Because they were originally *horns*."

The ram's horn reminds us of Abraham, who was willing to sacrifice his son, Isaac, unto G-d, until the boy was spared moments before the fatal blow and a ram substituted in his place. Thus, we use a musical instrument to commemorate the man who was not only the first Jew, but the first patriarch in history to be "punk'd" by G-d. No wonder the Jewish tradition is so rich in both comedy and music, and why so many Jews end up doing musical comedy.

What is the difference between a *shofar* and a trumpet? Traditionally, the person who blows the *shofar* (whose Hebrew designation can be translated—really—as "master blaster") is a man of special piety and purity of conduct, while the man who blows the trumpet is Miles Davis.

There are three sounds specific to the *shofar*'s ritual use. They are:

- the *tekiah* (pl., *tekiot*)—a deep blast that ends suddenly
- the *teruah*—a trill between two *tekiot*
- the *shevarim*—three connected short sounds

There is also the *tekiah gadolah*, or "big *tekiah*," which is an extended *tekiah*.

Out of these three sounds one constructs the traditional ten *tekiot*, repeated three times, for the thirty sounds required for the Holy Day service. They are played in this order: *tekiah*; *shevarim-teruah*; *tekiah*; *tekiah-shevarim-tekiah*; *tekiah-teruah-tekiah*, ending with *tekiah gadolah*.

With a little practice, these primitive but awe-inspiring sounds can be extended, modulated, and recombined into the following horn classics as recorded by the famous Jewish trumpet player Herb Alpert:

- "Spanish Flea"
- "The Lonely Bull"
- "Tijuana Taxi"
- "A Taste of Honey"
- "Rise"

Note that, to obtain the full effect, you'll have to multitrack the *shofar* parts.

50

FIVE PICKLES EVERY JEW
SHOULD KNOW FROM

ickles form an important part of a balanced diet for Jews, along with pastrami, cheesecake, a nice brisket, and maybe a little *schnecken* for dessert. The question is why, especially today, when using pickling as a preservative isn't as necessary as it was in the days before Frigidaires.

Jews love pickles for these reasons:

a. They taste good.
b. The acidity and general all-around zestiness of pickles goes well with fatty foods such as deli meats, brisket, and chicken.
c. A lot of Jewish cooking (i.e., provincial cuisine from Eastern Europe and Russia) has, apart from its occasional use of horseradish, not much use for heat or hot peppers and can often be somewhat bland. (Compare the recipes in a Jewish cookbook with the foods of Italy, Southeast Asia, India, China, Mexico, Africa, and South America.) Pickles perk things up.

The term "pickle" is a broad one. Readers seeking to become really Jewish should be aware that the following kinds of pickles, while of course delicious, are not especially Jewish:

• French cornichons
• Bread-and-butter pickles

- Those little ones, what do you call them, with the name like those British soldiers in India. Gherkins.
- Sweet pickles
- Those neon-green acidic disks that come on fast-food hamburgers
- Italian *giardiniera*
- Pickled okra
- Pickled garlic
- Pickled cherry peppers, "sport" peppers, chili peppers, etc.
- Indian lime pickle, mango pickle, etc.
- Kimchi
- Anything else not mentioned below

From the Jewish perspective, the five essential pickles (in order of importance) are:

1. Pickled cucumbers, or pickles
2. Pickled herring
3. Sauerkraut
4. Pickled tomatoes
5. Pickled onions

Indeed, so essential are these five that you can often get two or three of them (cucumbers; sauerkraut; tomatoes) *just by walking into a decent deli and sitting down at a table.* Somebody—a total stranger—brings them to you in a little metal dish. It's unbelievable.

It is essential, if you're going to perk up your flagging, deracinated sense of your own Jewishness, that you renew your acquaintance with the Five Pickles, and maybe think—it won't kill you to *think*—about making them at home yourself.

1. Pickled cucumbers. These are, of course, pickles. (Get this: The cucumber is a *fruit*. Like the tomato. Go know!) The term "kosher dill pickles" does not refer to *kashruth* (i.e., the Orthodox rules of keeping kosher); pickles that really are strictly kosher are labeled that way separately. By now "kosher" just means prepared as

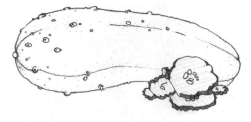

Actual drawing of pickle.

the Jews in New York City do it, by adding a good *zetz* (punch) of garlic. The pickling liquid in this case is brine, i.e., no vinegar. Kosher dills are pretty easy to make, actually, if you follow this recipe:

Pretty-Easy-to-Make Kosher Dill Pickles

2 qts. water
3 tbsp. coarse white salt (kosher, if available)
9–10 kirby cucumbers, scrubbed
4 cloves garlic, unpeeled and lightly, cursorily crushed
1 tbsp. pickling spice augmented with ¼ tsp. fennel seed (or
    anise seed, but maybe a little less) and ¼ tsp. celery seed.
    (For zippy-peppy thrills, add a small dried hot chili
    pepper broken in half. Keep the seeds for more heat,
    or discard them.)

3 large or 4 medium bay leaves
1 small bunch of dill, washed and kind of roughed up in your
    fingers to get it exuding dillness.

*NOTE: You will be fascinated to learn that kosher salt is
not salt that somehow, through rabbinic or divine interven-
tion, has become kosher. It's coarse salt used for koshering.
Don't use regular table salt, which is too salty. The smaller
crystals mean more surface area—just never mind. Use
kosher.*

1. In a large pot (stainless steel or aluminum; not cast iron) heat
about a third of the water with the salt until the salt is dissolved.
You don't have to boil it. Add the remaining water; stir.

2. Prepare two or three jars wide enough to accommodate the
cukes snugly, thus: Either fill them with boiling water and then
pour it out, or run them through a full cycle in a dishwasher.

3. Pack the cucumbers vertically (duh) into the jars, dividing
the garlic, spices, bay leaves, and dill among them as you go. You
might try filling one jar with cukes sliced into spears, which will
pickle more quickly.

4. Fill the jars with the brine so that the cucumbers are completely immersed. Cover the jars with cheesecloth secured with
rubber bands, or loosely with the lids. You want some air to find
its way into them. Store in a cool, dark place for three days. "Cool"
means lower than room temperature, not "groovy." Don't store
your pickles in a boutique or a dance club.

5. You may be wondering, "Okay, but will there be scum?"
Probably not, but if there is, just spoon it out. Don't be a baby.
After three days—two days with spears—taste a pickle. The whole
fermentation process will generally be from three to six days. The
longer you let them go, the more sour they'll become. Once you
like how they taste, put the jars into the refrigerator.

2. Pickled herring. Beloved of Jews from Russia, and of Jews from Scandinavia, if there are any, and of non-Jews from Scandinavia, and of non-Jews from Russia, if there are any. And the Dutch, who invented a marinated dish called "soused herring" or *rollmops,* for which the process known as *gibbing* is ge—

Wait. Do we have to get into this? Just bear in mind that you cure the herring in salt (if it hasn't been salted yet) or fresh water, then make fillets, cut them into pieces, boil a marinade of water, vinegar, and spices (including sugar), and let the pieces soak for three days. Serve with (ugh) lingonberries if you're Swedish, which, let's face it, you're not, or sour cream (yum) if you're Jewish, and onions no matter what.

There is also chopped herring, which consists of pickled herring that has been chopped. Ashkenazi Jews give it the not-so-tempting name *forshmak* salad, but they have their reasons. It's mushy, but you might like it on a nice cracker. That's your business.

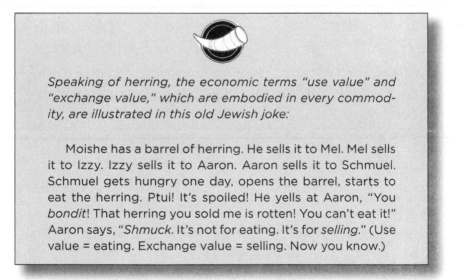

Speaking of herring, the economic terms "use value" and "exchange value," which are embodied in every commodity, are illustrated in this old Jewish joke:

Moishe has a barrel of herring. He sells it to Mel. Mel sells it to Izzy. Izzy sells it to Aaron. Aaron sells it to Schmuel. Schmuel gets hungry one day, opens the barrel, starts to eat the herring. Ptui! It's spoiled! He yells at Aaron, "You *bondit*! That herring you sold me is rotten! You can't eat it!" Aaron says, *"Shmuck.* It's not for eating. It's for *selling."* (Use value = eating. Exchange value = selling. Now you know.)

3. Sauerkraut. German for "sour cabbage." Okay, so you knew that. But did you happen to know that a nutritionist at King's College, London, did a study that revealed that pickled cabbage is as effective as Viagra at increasing sexual function? Lejla Kazinic Kreho is the lady who made this inspiring discovery, which she reported in her book *Nutrition of the 21st Century.*

Many cuisines have their own form of sour cabbage, but being German makes it especially Jewish. It is, of course, an essential ingredient in the Reuben sandwich—not to mention on hot dogs.

By the way, here's a recipe that's so easy it's not even a recipe. It's just something to do to cabbage to make it good.

Something to Do to Cabbage to Make It Good

1 head red cabbage, trimmed of the outer horrible leaves
white vinegar
water
a jar

1. Cut a hunk of the cabbage off and slice it into nice, bite-size chunks. Fill the jar about two-thirds of the way with them.

2. Create a solution of one-half white vinegar and one-half water. Pour in over the cabbage until it's all immersed.

3. Close the jar and put in the fridge and walk away.

4. Period.

5. Taste it the next day and you will find that not only has the liquid turned a delightful purple but the cabbage will be tart

and fresh and unbelievably crunchy. You can put some salt in when you are making it, or salt it as you eat it.

6. Augment this with a) sliced carrots; b) a sprig of dill or rosemary; c) a little black pepper; d) a sliced jalapeño pepper; or, of course, e) a crushed garlic clove. But you really don't need to. White cabbage works, too, but because its leaves are thinner, it doesn't come out as unbelievably crunchy.

Will this stimulate sexual function as well as Viagra? Look, it doesn't matter. What matters is how unbelievably crunchy it is.

4. Pickled tomatoes. What is so Jewish about pickled tomatoes? They're part of the repertoire of pickled items common to many Eastern European cuisines. The art of pickling tomatoes is . . . well, first of all, it's not an art. Making a nice painting or sculpture is an art. Making pickled tomatoes is more like a skill.

To pickle green tomatoes all you do is parboil them, then stack them in jars and cover with a marinade consisting of water, vinegar, sugar, and spices. They're ready the next day.

And they're available under Jewish labels in your grocer's pickle case, which sounds more pornographic than maybe it should.

5. Pickled onions. Also easy, also great. And indispensable, not only in martinis, but with pickled herring, on grilled meats, and with everything else except ice cream. You brine onions in salt water, then cover them with a marinade in a sterilized jar for five weeks or more. Big onions, little onions, red onions, whatever. The point is: There are various ways of being a really Jewish Jew that maybe aren't so fun, like building an ark, but making and eating pickles is almost completely fun. So you have to wash some dishes afterward. Big deal.

51

FLAUNT CONTRADICTORY OPINIONS
ABOUT THE AFTERLIFE!

The afterlife (or the World to Come, the translation of the traditional Hebrew *Olam Ha-Ba*) is the trickiest concept in all of Judaism. When the subject comes up, scholars and rabbis and authors all get cute. They become allegorical and evasive and metaphorical, and you keep wanting to say, "Yeah, okay, but wait. Are you saying . . ."

There is, in Judaism, the opposite of unanimity regarding the afterlife. There's even a complete lack of consensus as to whether Judaism has a concept of the afterlife at all. There are terms for Heaven (*Gan Eden*—the Garden of Eden; Paradise) and Hell (*Gehinnom*). But a strong scholarly and doctrinal tradition holds that these are metaphors, and not to be taken with crass literalness as places you do or don't get sent to after death. In this view, virtue and righteousness are their own reward, not ways to accumulate credits to qualify for fabulous prizes.

Then again, many Orthodox authorities who dismiss the possibility of an otherworldly afterlife do, nonetheless, believe in the eventual appearance of the Messiah. That's what they mean by the World to Come: a time of universal peace and social justice, to be ushered in by a human chosen by G-d to redeem mankind.

The Messiah aside, ask ten Jews what they believe about life after death and most of them will probably say not only that they don't know what to think, but that they don't know what they're *supposed* to think.

You might be tempted to read this and throw up your hands and say, "Great. Five thousand years of intense theological discussion, with the writings and the commentaries and the marginalia and the Talmudic passages making footnotes about the footnotes, winding around and around in an endless river of discourse and hairsplitting and speculation . . . All that, and they can't agree on one of the most basic tenets a religion can have."

It's frustrating and disappointing, yes. But you have to admire Judaism's unwillingness to make promises it can't keep or that G-d never actually made.

A symbolic depiction of Heaven and Hell, neither of which Jews literally believe in.

Thus, if you want to flaunt your newly traditional (i.e., agnostic!) Jewish view of the afterlife, simply go up to the people you want to impress and say the following:

1. Jews don't really believe in the objective, literal existence of Heaven or Hell, but—
2. —some do, although the idea that Heaven and Hell are actual places (or even states of being) is probably a remnant of primitive folklore used to illustrate the consequences of righteousness and evil to less sophisticated people in previous eras, but bear in mind that—
3. —Jews also don't really believe in actually saying they *don't* really believe in Heaven or Hell, and in any case—
4. —it's all a metaphor designed to encourage people to live ethically here and now, creating a Paradise on earth, although—
5. —we're not sure. We say "G-d doesn't create Paradise; people do," although the question, "What good is a religion if it doesn't at least guarantee an afterlife?"—
6. —is a good, albeit rhetorical, question, and probably good for another five thousand years' worth of discussion.

Better yet, skip it. Change the subject and talk about how you always fast on Yom Kippur. That's impressive. Everybody knows what it's like to be hungry.

52

A (JEWISH) STAR IS BORN
The Magen David

In your quest to feel and act and be more Jewish, you may be tempted to use the "Jewish star" as a substitute for a "normal" five-pointed star. For example, instead of this:

TUESDAY

✡   Ask Leslie re doughnuts
PICK UP LIZARDS!!!
✡   Trig Final—>skip?
APPENDECTOMY TOMORROW! Fast night before!

. . . you might decide to write and draw this:

✡   Ask Leslie re doughnuts
PICK UP LIZARDS!!!
✡   Trig Final—>skip?
APPENDECTOMY TOMORROW! Fast night before!

And why not? After all, they're both stars. And why not use it in posters, ads, letterhead, logos, and any other graphic image where otherwise you'd use a five-pointed star? Right?

Well . . . It depends. You can obviously use whatever symbols you like in creating your own private graphics for your own private self and family and friends. But the Jewish star is not just a-star-with-six-points-instead-of-five. It's not only the Jewish star, it's the *Jewish* star, with all the history and *tsurris* and triumph and tragedy that entails.

The *Magen* David (also Star of David and, confusingly, Shield of David, which refers to Jewish prayers to G-d) is, today, the official symbol of the State of Israel. It's on the Israeli flag and the jets in the Israeli air force, etc., and is universally acknowledged to mean "Jewish," and all. However!

Interestingly, this hexagram wasn't always synonymous with Jews.

Until the Middle Ages, the symbol most often used for that purpose was—are you sitting down?—the *menorah*. What kind of a symbol of a brave, plucky, etc. people is a candelabra? As a universal symbol for Liberace, okay. But for the Jews?

That came to an end sometime in the Middle Ages, when the Kabbalists adopted it as a central motif on talismans and amulets. Since then it's remained as the most recognizable symbol of Judaism—both for better (when used by everyone except Nazis and other anti-Semites) and worse (when used by Nazis and other anti-Semites).

Using it as your own personal doodle-signifier for "important" is similar to dotting your i's with a heart or a little circle. "Creative," maybe, but in a pushy, willed, adolescent way, and kind of dippy in its desperation to be artistic or fun or, in this case, "really Jewish." So use a star when you need a star. Use the Jewish star wherever you would use a Jewish star.

53

HUMILITY NOW!

Seriously: What's the deal with humility?

As a Jewish ethical value it is fundamental. Sure, we all loved Charlton Heston's nostril-flaring, declamatory Moses in *The Ten Commandments*, but the "real" Moses (whatever that means) is described in the Bible as "meek." Hillel, twelve centuries later, also became an admired symbol of humility, to the point where "humble, like Hillel" became a figure of speech.

Humility was prized as the essential trait of the wise man, the *chacham*, whose sagacity everyone aspired to and revered. The sages themselves praised humility with such sayings as "Do not forget that G-d created the flea before he made man," and "Any man who thinks himself superior to his fellow man is really inferior to him."

It may be that every religion tells its adherents to be humble, since everyone is, by definition, inferior to and subservient to G-d. But, as their status as a persecuted and disdained minority grew, Jews had a social reason for being, if not modest, then certainly discreet about promoting themselves in public. (See chapter 25, "Chillin' and Illin' With *Tefillin*," for a mention of the fourth-century shift from openly wearing phylacteries out and about, and thus advertising one's Jewishness, to restricting their use to private moments at home and in synagogue.) Who knows to what extent declining to present yourself as a

Jew resulted in declining to present yourself as a person—and was made a virtue because of its necessity?

But when you think of Jews in America you don't think of humility. As we say in Yiddish, *Au contraire*. You think of self-assertion, achievement, and fame. You think of Nobel Prizes and showbiz luminaries and painters and sculptors, Jewish senators, congressmen, governors, Supreme Court justices, corporate titans, well-known scholars, and sports-team owners, plus a swarm of folk, rock, pop, and jazz stars including Beck, Pink, half of KISS, all of Simon and Garfunkel, and the entire J. Geils Band except, literally, J. Geils.

It's not that comparing the social behavior of Jews in late twentieth- and early twenty-first-century America to that of their forebears in medieval (or 1930s) Europe is unfair. The fact that things were much worse then and are much better now, in terms of the public "acceptance" of Jews, *is the point*. No Jew today is forced to hide. So why, again, should we be humble?

Add to all that the "psychologizing" of the middle class that followed World War II, and the idea of Moses-like, Hillelian meekness seems not only for losers from Squaresville, but actually bad for your health. Isn't it pathological to feel (or to think you should feel) that you're not important? Isn't it self-defeating, self-limiting, and neurotic? Isn't shyness a symptom of low self-esteem? How, unless you step forward and open up a mouth, can you get what you want and what you need?

That's the American in us talking. And who can blame it? In the United States today, competition for everything seems to have been amped up. Now it's kill or be killed, eat or be eaten, flaunt or be overshadowed, assert or be ignored. This may or may not be true for Hasidim, but for the more secular rest of us, aggressiveness and self-assertiveness seem less like matters of personal style and more like matters of personal survival.

So, fine. But bear in mind that the more you do that, the less Jewish you feel.

The more avid your pursuit of me-first egotism, the more assimilated by the secular, go-for-it, all-American consumer society Borg you

become. When Jews valued humility, it was not only to assure a low profile in an anti-Semitic society. It was also because, as a people who valued Torah, study, and learning, they knew that everyone was rendered
humble by what they didn't know. If praiseworthiness resides in obtaining knowledge and wisdom, then nobody is a big shot, because nobody
can know enough to qualify. There's always more that you haven't read,
haven't learned, haven't debated, and haven't mastered.

"No, please—no praise. I didn't write them. I just wrote
them *down*."

Humility, then, is a Jewish trait exactly to the extent that pizzazz and *chutzpah* and egotism are American traits. The table below will help you learn to convert the one into the other—to take a brief vacation, as it were, from your hard-charging American identity and spend a little time in your modest, self-abnegating, traditionally Jewish self.

For half an hour every day, practice replacing the kinds of aggressive, self-asserting things you might normally say (listed in the column "The Kinds of Aggressive, Self-Assertive Things You Might Normally Say") with modest sentiments of humility and self-effacement (noted under the column so designated).

Humility Substitution Table

Triggering Remark	The Kinds of Aggressive, Self-Assertive Things You Might Normally Say	Modest Sentiments of Humility and Self-Effacement
That's the most brilliant idea I've ever heard!	Hey, that was my idea!	I don't remember who came up with it. I guess we all did.
What a beautiful home you have!	I designed and decorated it myself, you know.	I'm glad you feel so comfortable.
This is the most amazing meal I've ever eaten!	It should be. I slaved all day.	Oh, I just follow the recipe. I'm glad you like it.
I can't believe you made the deadline!	I can't either. I worked my ass off.	Well, I didn't do it alone. I'm part of a terrific team.
You broke up with him/her? Oh no!	I had to. He/she was driving me nuts.	He/she is wonderful. We just weren't right for each other.

Triggering Remark	The Kinds of Aggressive, Self-Assertive Things You Might Normally Say	Modest Sentiments of Humility and Self-Effacement
You have such a great sense of style.	I really do. Thanks.	Really? That's sweet of you to say. I just buy stuff.
You give the best advice.	That's because I'm the only sane one around here.	I'm sorry—I have a tendency to stick my nose where it doesn't belong.

Will it help? Look, it couldn't hurt. Besides, in Jewish tradition, while it's always virtuous to give *tzedaka* (charity), the truest charitable spirit resides in those who give it without seeking acknowledgment or credit for it. Virtue—how crazy is this?—resides in anonymity.